The NLP Cookbook

The NLP Cookbook

50 Life Enhancing NLP Techniques for Coaches, Therapists and Trainers

Fran Burgess

Crown House Publishing Ltd
www.crownhouse.co.uk
www.crownhousepublishing.com

First published by

Crown House Publishing Ltd
Crown Buildings, Bancyfelin, Carmarthen, Wales, SA33 5ND, UK
www.crownhouse.co.uk

and

Crown House Publishing Company LLC
6 Trowbridge Drive, Suite 5, Bethel, CT 06801, USA
www.crownhousepublishing.com

British Library of Cataloguing-in-Publication Data
A catalogue entry for this book is available from the British Library.

Print ISBN 9781845907334
Mobi ISBN 9781845908414
ePub ISBN 9781845908422

LCCN 20011937941

Printed and bound in the UAE by
Oriental Press, Dubai

Contents

Introduction

You are in for such a treat.

This NLP Cookbook will appeal to the NLP diner within you. Whether you are already using Neurolinguistic Programming to explore with friends and family or you are working professionally with NLP as a manager, coach, trainer or therapist, you are certain to discover much here to support your practice. Even if you have just been introduced to NLP, you will find ways to stretch your thinking and extend your skills. How far you take it is down to you.

Why a 'cookbook'? I have been thinking about how techniques are constructed for a few years now, and every time I began to explain what I wanted to do, I would resort to a cooking metaphor as the simplest explanation – which is all very strange given that culinary skills are not high on my list of accomplishments!

NLP is known for its techniques. In fact, NLP is often described as a toolkit offering unique tools for different purposes. Whilst NLP is much more than this, it certainly is true that NLP techniques can deliver extraordinarily powerful experiences. You will no doubt have many stories of your own to back this up. Yet the range of tools to choose from is still fairly limited – even after 40 years – and most are found within the basic NLP repertoire. Few new techniques have made their way to the marketplace. The danger is that this can leave many practitioners with a feeling of 'what now?' before moving off to pastures new.

Now you are about to be spoilt for choice. As a result of a really simple model I devised, I am delighted to offer you this collection of original 'recipes', with supportive commentary and materials. Your Explorers will have even more opportunity to extend their flexibility, improve their relationships and work towards their goals.

All the recipes have been tested, and modified, as a result of the feedback I've received. I have also tested each of them myself – a fascinating personal journey, let me tell you. In fact, I can't recommend this process highly enough, although I say so myself! The feedback has been really satisfying.

It is great to dip into. There may be a particular exercise I can use for a course, or I may just take the approach and adapt it to what I'm doing.
A trainer

I used one of the exercises the next day with a client, and it worked tremendously well. I was really glad I had a copy.
A therapist

There was a particular issue that I was wanting to resolve. I took several of the techniques and worked through them. It was remarkable what emerged and how easy it was.
A learner

We have begun to use these recipes in our practice group as a way of directing our skills. It is refreshing to get our hands on new materials. When's the next one due?
An NLP practitioner

The Recipes

The recipes on offer deal with different problem areas. Quite a few focus on how to shift state, with some of these targeting specific states like acceptance and anxiety. These are followed by recipes that seek to develop behaviours and skills, and others that address beliefs and identity. You have a wide range of recipes to choose from which deal with goals, relationships and the process of change. The beauty is that most of them can be used time and again for different circumstances and contexts, so they never wear out.

As the Guide, your job is to take your Explorer through the process. To help you, each recipe is prefaced by an introduction which gives some background to its source and evolution. You are then provided with the ingredients: the level of skill required to get the most from the process, those involved – the Explorer and/or the Guide – plus timings and resources required. For the technically minded, details of the construction are given.

The instructions are written as a script for you to read directly to your Explorer. Sometimes you are offered some additional direction and supportive comment, alongside your Explorer's instructions. Some of these techniques don't need a Guide. If this is the case, then the Explorer can work independently, at his or her own pace, keeping the process private and spontaneous.

Where some of the techniques require your Explorer to walk into different spaces, if you have enough room, you'll get a far richer experience if you allow them to do this.

I strongly suggest that you follow the structure of the questions as they are written, since they are constructed for a purpose – to take your Explorer's attention to a particular place. However, if you have a streak of burning independence and choose to go your own way, all will not be lost. You will certainly generate something new and, who knows, it may make for an even more powerful and useful experience.

Novice cooks, like me, tend to follow recipes slavishly, knowing that disaster lies just behind the sloppy measuring or omission of an ingredient. However, there are cooks who earn my undying admiration and envy who can intuitively adapt a recipe, adding a little something here, removing a little something there. This is not magic. They understand the chemistry that underpins the cooking process. They know what happens when you put this with that, now or later – a wisdom still to be gained where I'm concerned in the kitchen!

And so it may be with you. You might already have lots of NLP experience and are able to adapt processes to address whatever is emerging for your Explorer. If you, as the Guide, want to add a different twist in response to your Explorer's awareness, please feel free. If, however, you don't have these skills yet it is wiser to stick with the stages as they appear.

Some of the techniques highlight the need for advanced levels of skill. If, as a beginner, you attempt them then it is unlikely you will attain the desired results. Whilst your Explorer will instinctively know how to protect him or herself from your relative lack of skill, it is best not to put them in that position in the first place. For this same reasoning, I leave making flaky pastry and soufflé to the experts there is only so much my friends' digestion should be expected to tolerate!

Future Applications

There are some people who can read a recipe and know exactly how the dish is likely to taste. So some of you may be able to skim through this book and already be aware of the potential experiences on offer.

If you have a particular goal in mind, a targeted audience or a specific problem that needs addressing, then you are likely to find at least two or three recipes that will fit your purpose immediately, or ones that can be easily adapted. In Appendix 2 you will find a comprehensive table recording the model type, the delivery method, linguistic and neurological frames used for each recipe, so you can quickly select those that suit your purposes. Who knows, you could find yourself looking at a ready-made workshop! Glad to be of service.

And it won't take long for you to realise that ingredients, models and processes can be chopped and changed. Once you have mastered cooking your model in the Provençal sauce of say submodalities + time, you can opt to place a different model into this mix. Conversely, you may choose to take your model and give it a different treatment, cooking it with triple description and mentors instead. Whilst there are 50 recipes here, you have at your fingertips many more – opening the door to a mind-blowing potential repertoire, which is never-ending.

Honour Your Sources

You are welcome to take these techniques out into the wider world – there is no point in keeping them to yourself. If you do, and I would be delighted if you did, then I ask only one thing:

Honour your sources.

If you find yourself including any of this material formally or informally into your work, I ask that you name the source and the originator. Similarly, if this material has inspired you to want to develop a process further, then claim your place as the developer and reference the source. In this way we can maintain the fabulous lineage we have been given in a respectful and honourable manner.

Feedback

Whilst all the recipes in *The NLP Cookbook* have been tested thoroughly, everyone is different and unique. If you find that a particular process didn't work for you or your Explorer, then I would be really interested to learn what happened and what you did. Whilst I think I have been realistic about skill level requirements, I may be guilty of being over-optimistic. Anyway do let me know, by emailing me – fran@nlpand.co.uk.

Personal Review

You may choose to go through these recipes as part of your personal development, which I would really recommend. Decide how you want to record your work. You may be happy to work directly onto your computer or you may prefer writing by hand, either on loose paper or in a journal bought specially for this journey. You may identity a particular format and stick to that for each day's work. You may select one exercise a day or do as many as you have time for that morning. Personally, I preferred to feel free to write as little or as much as I wanted. I also found that other conversations were emerging as a result of the exercises, which I also recorded.

Along the way natural punctuation points emerged when I would stop and reflect on the significant insights and emergent themes. I didn't want to lose the gems that were presenting themselves. I wished to keep tabs on my discoveries and to make myself accountable for them as well.

So taking time to stop and review really consolidates your learning and rewards your commitment to your process of self-discovery. To this end, I am suggesting you record the following elements:

1 Date
2 You may also want to include what else has been happening to you that day/week to provide context
3 Technique – number/title
4 Answers to questions
5 Key insights
6 Emerging themes
7 Emerging outcomes
8 Identified actions

And Finally

I do hope this book fuels your appreciation of NLP. I would be heartened to learn that it inspires you to further reading, takes you to a practice group or finds you registering for more training.

NLP is an area of practice that has to be used and experienced before it comes alive. Learning about it and knowing the theory is like keeping cookery books on your coffee table. A dog-eared recipe book is a thing of joy, as it conjures up all the people who have enjoyed the benefits of the cooking. These recipes are offered to be consumed, again and again, for all your Explorers to come.

Enjoy. Have fun with your discoveries. And raise a glass to the many thinkers and developers who have made this possible for you.

Guidance Notes

Being a Guide your gift is to give your Explorer your full attention, so that in turn he or she can focus solely on what is happening for them, This means that you are not overly distracted by reading the next instruction or worrying about how you are doing.

If you are a relative newcomer to NLP, then you might like familiarise yourself with these guidelines. Even if you are an experienced practitioner, it is worth reminding yourself yet again of how to be with your Explorer.

1 The Explorer determines what happens in the exploration. All the information lies within the Explorer, not the sheet of paper holding the instructions.

2 A recipe or written instructions are merely an idealised account of what to do. If the Explorer doesn't seem to fit the recipe, then no amount of shoehorning will make it better. Either abandon the process and go on to something else, or if as a Guide you are particularly skilled, go with other options and see what more usefully emerges.

3 This is not a social situation. Your feelings and wellbeing are of no relevance to the Explorer. Gently dissuade your Explorer from the need to seek reassurance from you, and to break eye contact. Encourage him or her to trust in their own internal responses.

4 Resist the urge to talk about whatever comes up and suppress your nosiness.

Let your Explorer be free to explore uninterrupted by your opinions.

5 You may want to record the Explorer's words so that you can use them as auditory anchors and refer to them during the process.

6 Go at your Explorer's pace. Wait till your Explorer fully focuses on the outside world and seems ready to move on. Only then introduce the next question or next step.

7 Resist the desire to rescue. Tears can be a sign that your Explorer is touching on something important. Stay with it, and you will reap the rewards. Rushing in with a paper hankie, believe it or not, is hindering not helping! (It is more likely to be about you wanting to make yourself feel better.)

8 At the same time, your job is to keep your Explorer resourceful. If your Explorer becomes overwhelmed, you know the remedy is simple. Invite him or her to step out of the situation, and ask him or her to literally give a shake or look up at something, preferably some way off.

9 Always check that your Explorer desires the outcome the technique is offering and is happy to go through the process. Really look out for any signs of incongruence. Your Explorer may feel obligated to go down a particular route or be putting pressure on themselves.

10 Avoid getting out of your depth. Your Explorer may have chosen a particularly difficult topic. Remember to stay resourceful yourself and know that you can refer on. Most of the time your Explorer knows how to keep safe – the number of 'don't knows' are usually a bit of a clue.

11 Finally, use the calibration process wisely. Each technique offers a before and after scale. If there is not much improvement, then you may want to go back and revisit some of the stages on the way.

12 And finally know you can be tender, fierce and playful as you support Explorers in attaining priceless information about themselves.

The Recipes

The Recipes

The Treats in Store

You will find this collection of techniques sorted under their purpose, so that you can quickly go to the ones that most suit your needs. Hopefully this will direct your searches and also help you to select a combination of techniques to meet an overall goal.

The techniques are grouped under the following eight headings:

- State: general and specific
- Behaviours and skills
- Beliefs
- Identity
- Goals
- Relationships
- Change

Information Chart

THE INGREDIENTS
The Purpose
Description
The Conditions
Time, resources, who, skill level
The Delivery Method
Kinaesthetic, auditory, visual, cognitive
The NLP Frames
Neurological, linguistic

You'll notice that each recipe carries a table of information (like the one to the left) giving some details about how to work with it, as well as letting you know what is included to allow it to create the effects it does. This technical information is for the NLP techies amongst you, so don't be put off if it doesn't resonate with you.

1 The State Booster

Technique devised by Fran Burgess

This is a delightful and insightful process that came to me whilst I was on a workshop run by Judith Lowe and Judith DeLozier. It enables us to self-model and retrieve our own internal wisdom that is there for the asking.

THE INGREDIENTS

The Purpose
Suitable for developing a desired state

The Conditions
Time: 20 mins
Resources: None
Who: G + E
Skill Level: Easy

The Delivery Method
Cognitive: Questions

The NLP Frames
Neurological: Metaphor, mentor
Linguistic: Meta Model

I was exploring 'power' and what I believed about it, since I've been having a running conversation with the nature of power off and on for most of my life. Tying in with experiences I had with another changework process (actually the 'Stuff Happens' technique in Recipes 17 and 18) I identified that for me power was like the Gherkin building in London – don't ask me why! Once I had established this, I then knew I had thoughts about buildings – as does Norman Foster its designer and creator. So the process was born.

Your Explorer can choose any state that he or she would like to understand further. As the Guide, record all their responses word for word. If you're working on your own, note down your thoughts as you go along.

Those of you in the know will recognise that this is based on the use of metaphor and a couple of modal operators from the Meta Model framework.

20 MIN   G + E   EASY

The Technique

1   Think of a situation that is coming up
for you when you would like to be more
of a particular state – for example,
confidence or assertiveness.

The Explorer can choose
any state he or she wants.

2   As you think of this event:

■ How much [state] do you
currently have in this situation?
(1 low–10 high)

3   Now think back to a time when you felt
the state that you're looking for here.
Make sure you select one that fits for
the situation you're facing – you don't
want to over- or underdo it.

■ What metaphor sums up this feeling?
It is like … X.

Encourage your Explorer to trust his or her
instincts and go with the first idea that
comes up.

4   Taking this metaphor, answer each
statement with at least three responses
to each:

■ An X can be … it can be … and it can
be …

■ An X can't be … it can't be … and it
can't be …

■ An X doesn't have to be … or have to
be … or have to be …

■ An X does have to be … or has to
be … or has to be …

Write down your Explorer's answers.

5   Now, go to the creator of your
metaphor (if it was a building then you
would select the architect) and answer
the questions again:

■ An X can be … etc.

■ An X can't be … etc.

■ An X doesn't have to be … etc.

■ An X does have to be … etc.

6   Step fully into the metaphor and hear
your answers again.

Read out your Explorer's answers.

7   Imagine being in this situation once
more.

■ What are you doing and saying now?

■ What are others seeing and
experiencing?

■ What is your level of [state] now?

8   As you think of this event once more:

■ How much [state] do you now have in
this situation? (1 low–10 high)

2 The State Collage

Technique devised by Fran Burgess

This is another way to help your Explorers develop a desired state in a pleasing and simple way. It appeals to those who enjoy working with images and pictures. And if they don't, then this might just be your answer to jogging their system into becoming more alert, by activating a less habitual representation system.

THE INGREDIENTS

The Purpose
Suitable for developing a desired state

The Conditions
Time: 20 mins
Resources: Magazines, newspapers, pictures
Who: E
Skill Level: Easy

The Delivery Method
Visual: Collage

The NLP Frames
Neurological: Metaphor, time
Linguistic: Meta Model

It works on several levels. Your Explorers are physically involved in choosing images and so are combining touch with sight. They are working in the present and at the same time have an eye on the future. Within the structure of the technique, they are looking to bring past, present and future together to strengthen their internal understanding of what their chosen state means for them.

Then, by strategically placing the completed picture to catch their eye, they will be continuously tickling their unconscious mind as the picture continues to send its desirable message, leaving the unconscious mind to get on with the rest.

You could also consider asking them to combine sounds and work through the process in an auditory way, which might make for some interesting music!

The Technique

1 Think of a situation that is coming up for you, when you would like to be more, say, [patient]. This [X] is your desired state.

2 As you think of this event now:

 ■ How [X] are you feeling?
 (1 low–10 high)

3 Take your pile of magazines and begin to cut out images that somehow convey all the ways this state can be expressed.

> Encourage your Explorers to go with their 'waters', and trust their instincts!

4 If you can't find a particular image that you're looking for, then just sketch something yourself.

5 Begin to sort the pictures into three piles. You may find that you are moving images from one pile to another.

 ■ Pile 1: these images represent the level of [X] you know you have had.

 ■ Pile 2: these images represent the level of [X] you currently have.

 ■ Pile 3: these images represent the level of [X] you want to have.

6 Taking all your images, printed and hand drawn, lay them out on a sheet of A4 paper, placing 'old' [X] images on the left hand of the page, the current [X] images in the centre, and the 'new' type of [X] images on the right hand side. Once you have arranged them to your satisfaction, glue them into place.

7 As you do, make the following statements:

 ■ Having my [X] means I can …

 ■ Having my [X] means I am …

8 As you think of this event now:

 ■ How [X] are you feeling?
 (1 low–10 high)

9 Take your collage and put it where you will see it from time to time during the day. You might even scan it into your computer and make it your screensaver. When you see it, remind yourself of what your [X] means to you.

3 The Resource Builder

Technique devised by Judith DeLozier

Model devised by Robert Dilts

This seemingly simple process alerted me to the importance of understanding the dynamics between NLP ingredients. Based on Robert Dilts's SOAR (State, Operator and Result) Model, Judy has taken different perspectives and combined them with time. So simple and yet it delivers a powerful punch!

THE INGREDIENTS

The Purpose
Suitable for building and strengthening an emergent resource

The Conditions
Time: 30 mins
Resources: None
Who: G + E
Skill Level: Medium

The Delivery Method
Kinaesthetic: Spatial anchors

The NLP Frames
Neurological: Multiple perspectives, time
Linguistic: None

I can still remember my first experience of this process. My partner and I were under a palm tree in a quiet corner of the Balinese compound where we were training. I was bringing an infant sense of self-belief ready to grow and develop it. By the end of the process I had such a strong feeling of being a swan, with my arms involuntarily rising like wings. A tremendous amount has happened to me since then, and I suspect this swan may have made no small contribution. As an afterthought, it's only now as I write this that I am reminded that my imprinted fairy story was *The Ugly Duckling*! You may remember Danny Kaye's rendering of 'What me a swan? Aw go on!'

30 MIN   G + E   MEDIUM

The Technique

2nd Future	1st Future	3rd Future
2nd Present	1st Present	3rd Present
2nd Past	1st Past	3rd Past

1   Become aware of a resource which is beginning to grow inside of you.

■ How strong is your sense of this resource? (1 low–10 high)

■ What gesture or posture sums up your current feeling?

2   Following this sequence, go to each square and face the Present You. Gather whatever thoughts and information you are offered, no matter how strange it may initially sound. Ask your partner to record it. After each 'visit', return to the central square of 1st Present and hear the message you were given.

■ 1st Present: This is You today. Feel the resource within you. What is it like?

■ 1st Future: This is You some time in the future. What do you want to say to Present You?

Let your Explorer know to allow whatever the future or past time-period to emerge.

■ 2nd Future: Select someone who is experiencing You at this point in the future. What does this person say?

■ 3rd Future: Look at the relationship between the two of you in the future. What thought comes to mind?

■ 2nd Present: Select someone who is experiencing You today. What does this person say?

■ 3rd Present: Look at the relationship between the two of you from here. What thought comes to mind?

■ 1st Past: This is You at some point in the past. What do you want to say?

■ 2nd Past: Select someone who is experiencing You at this point in the past. What does this person say?

■ 3rd Past: Look at the relationship between the two of you from here. What thoughts come to mind?

Warn your Explorer against trying to second-guess it.

3   Staying in the centre, once all messages have been received, ask your partner to walk around you, reading out the messages in no particular order. If you want, you can be moving round in the opposite direction.

4   Finally, become aware now of the strength of your resource.

■ How strong is your sense of this resource? (1 low–10 high)

■ What gesture or posture sums up your current feeling?

4 Safety and Vulnerability

Technique devised by Fran Burgess

Based on work by Milton Erickson

This is an example of a simple technique that has been created by taking two elements from a larger model – in this instance the Independence Model encompassing the values of power, control, vulnerability and safety. Recipes 15 and 16 use this model as well. It is fascinating just how much you can do with merely two elements.

THE INGREDIENTS

The Purpose
Suitable for enabling more choice in uncomfortable situations

The Conditions
Time: 30 mins
Resources: None
Who: G + E
Skill Level: Medium

The Delivery Method
Cognitive: Relational constructs
Kinaesthetic: Spatial anchors

The NLP Frames
Neurological: None
Linguistic: None

First of all, as a way of stretching out the problem space, your Explorers are invited to examine the extremes of each of the values, in terms of what they mean for them. In this way they may find themselves exploring beyond the existing limits to their thinking.

Then with some of their thinking now loosened up, they are swirled around in the ambiguity and confusion of contrasting constructs by mixing the wording to create different effects. Milton Erickson, the master of hypnotic trance, would use this sort of approach in what he called the Confusion Technique. It results in the conscious mind giving up the effort of making sense of what was being said, so letting the unconscious mind have its insightful way.

30 MIN   G + E   MEDIUM

The Technique

Vulnerably safe	**Safely safe**
Safely vulnerable	**Vulnerably vulnerable**

1 Think of a situation where you are hesitant and fire on few of your cylinders. It might be with people or a location or activity.

   ■ How safe do you feel?
   (1 low–10 high)

   ■ How exposed do you feel?
   (1 low–10 high)

2 Before you explore this situation further, consider the following questions:

   ■ What happens if you stay safe all the time?

   ■ What happens if you are never safe?

   ■ What happens when you are totally exposed?

   ■ What happens when you are completely protected?

3 Using your situation, step into each of the four spaces set out as above. In each space, ask yourself:

   ■ What is this like?

   ■ What happens?

4 Step into the middle of all four spaces:

   ■ What do you now know about safety and vulnerability?

   ■ How much of each do you really need in this situation?

5 Imagine you are about to enter into a situation similar to the one you have been exploring.

   ■ What preparations are you making?

   ■ What are you telling yourself?

   ■ What are you now going to be paying attention to?

   ■ How safe do you feel?
   (1 low–10 high)

   ■ How exposed do you feel?
   (1 low–10 high)

5 Sad to Glad

Technique devised by Fran Burgess

Based on work by Richard Bandler, John Grinder and Judith DeLozier

Way back in the early days of NLP, the process called Chaining Anchors was devised to enable changes in state. It worked on a couple of premises: (1) we can only hold a state for 90 seconds before it needs to be topped up by returning to whatever triggered it, and (2) if we can plummet from happy to sad on a sixpence, it suggests we can go in the opposite direction just as easily.

THE INGREDIENTS

The Purpose
Suitable for moving
to a useful state

The Conditions
Time: 20 mins
Resources: None
Who: G + E
Skill Level: Easy

The Delivery Method
Kinaesthetic: Somatic syntax,
spatial anchors

The NLP Frames
Neurological: None
Linguistic: None

However, the process is quite cumbersome and requires lots of tricky anchoring skills. Personally, I dislike any process that requires my physical intervention; I much prefer it if the Explorer can do all the work themselves. It seems more ecological and promotes greater autonomy and independence.

So I have dipped into Judith DeLozier's 'somatic dancing', where she uses the body to let us know what we need to do. Some of you may have already experienced this approach in Dancing the SCORE.

This set-up is rather like those word puzzles you get – change 'pond' into 'melt' in four steps by altering only one letter at a time. I have chosen the sad to glad polarity, but you could go for confused to certain, fearful to adventurous, or whatever is running for you at the moment. You don't have to go for just two interim states; however, I suggest you limit yourself to a maximum of seven steps.

Encourage your Explorers to take up their posture instinctively. Get them to listen to their body talking. This is *not* about acting sad or acting glad; it is about expressing what sad or glad feels like physically.

The Technique

1. Identify the state you don't want and the state you do want. Now in-between both come up with interim states that take you progressively from the first to the last. For example:

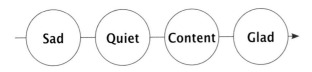

2. Place the progression of states in a line on the floor, giving yourself enough room to move between them.

3. Step into the first space and allow your body to adopt a posture that fits with that state. Avoid forcing and trust that the appropriate posture will emerge. If your head feels heavy, let it drop down. If your knees want to bend, it might be that you want to kneel down.

4. Once you have the posture make a note of it, so that you are certain you can reproduce it again. Then shake it off and move to the next one.

5. Go through all of the states to make sure you are clear about the posture you take up for each one.

6. You are now ready to 'dance' along your line, stringing the different postures together. You want to pay particular attention to the first body movement you make that takes you from one shape to the next. This can often give you a metaphorical clue: 'Take a deep breath' or 'Physically put one foot forward'.

7. Practise the transitions between the spaces a couple of times, and then dance freely from beginning to end.

8. Repeat several times.

9. At the final space, come up with a gesture that encapsulates the feeling you now have. Know that this can be your trigger to give yourself a boost as and when you need it.

6 Body Talk

Technique devised by Fran Burgess

This is another process that took me by surprise. Whilst not directly from within the NLP stable, it finds a comfortable home here since it is a different way of connecting with our unconscious mind and gathering information, which is hidden away in those nooks and crannies of our psyche.

THE INGREDIENTS

The Purpose
Suitable for easing stress and pain

The Conditions
Time: 30 mins
Resources: Personal journal
Who: E
Skill Level: Easy

The Delivery Method
Cognitive: Questions
Auditory: Writing

The NLP Frames
Neurological: Multiple perspectives
Linguistic: Meta Model

I was introduced to the idea of writing to a part of my body when I found myself in a party of esoteric tree-huggers high in the Andes of Chile. We were invited to write to our heart and then let our heart write back. The beauty that emerged, the wisdom and the lyricism that my words contained blew me away. I am now a total convert. After all, our emotions are stored in our body, and our mind connects throughout our neurology.

Recently I suggested this process to someone who has had a serious heart condition for a number of years. As a result, instead of seeing his heart as the enemy and something to overcome, he now takes on a more sponsoring role, coming alongside it and in the process understanding its purpose more fully. Arielle Essex of Performing Miracles describes how she went through a similar sponsoring process to help heal a brain tumour she once had.

Hand your Explorers a copy of the instructions for them to take away. Whilst the questions have been offered to stimulate thinking, let your Explorers feel free to let their thoughts have a mind of their own.

30 MIN

EASY

20

The Technique

1   Find a quiet place without distraction.

2   Be aware of what is troubling you. Where in your body do you keep this sense of trouble – your heart, stomach, throat, lungs? (You may have some physical symptoms.)

   ■ What is your level of stress/pain? (1 low–10 high)

3   Having identified that part of your body, begin to write to it, recording whatever you find yourself wanting to say. Just let your pen run until it comes to a complete stop.

4   To get you started, or if you run out of steam, you might like to consider:

   ■ How have I treated you?

   ■ What do I expect from you? What demands have I been making?

   ■ What should you be doing? How have you let me down?

   ■ What have I been ignoring? What will happen as a result?

   ■ What is our relationship like?

5   Once you have come to a full stop in your writing, start on a fresh page and invite that part of your body to write back to you. Again, let whatever words flow out from your pen to happen. But if you get stuck, you may want to consider, from the perspective of your body:

   ■ How do you want to be treated?

   ■ What will happen if the current situation continues?

   ■ What does it mean if the current situations continue? What else?

   ■ How would you like the relationship to continue?

   ■ What must never happen? What can happen instead?

6   You can continue this conversation until you find yourself arriving at some level of agreement and mutual accommodation.

   ■ What is your level of stress/pain now? (1 low–10 high)

7 The Accepting Process

Technique devised by Steve Gilligan

Adapted by Fran Burgess

Steve Gilligan, as part of his whole approach to sponsorship and inclusion, constantly seeks ways of achieving internal integration to help heal the division and fragmentation that has occurred during our early development process. He recognises that we live to hide those aspects of ourselves that we consider to be unworthy. And every time we do so, we continue to deny who we are and push the prospect of self-acceptance further into the future.

THE INGREDIENTS

The Purpose
Suitable for developing
self-acceptance

The Conditions
Time: 30 mins
Resources: Personal journal
Who: G + E
Skill Level: Medium

The Delivery Method
Cognitive: Questions

The NLP Frames
Neurological: None
Linguistic: Milton Model

I experienced the power of the first stage of this technique a few years ago and it made a huge impact on me. The edict that 'I am not my behaviour' really is proven to be true through this technique. However, at a later workshop with Steve, I realised that I had made even more progress. By presenting my 'vices' with confidence and congruence, I had strengthened my acceptance of them, and therefore reduced the need to trumpet my 'virtues'. Taking this further, and by accepting that I have absolutely no control over how another perceives me, the most powerful message I can offer is my own self-assurance and self-acceptance.

I hope this process works for your Explorers as well.

The Technique

1. Identify at least four things that you are proud of about yourself (A) and four that you would rather keep hidden (B).

2. Round 1: Select a partner and turn about go through the following process for each of your four pairs of attributes.

   ■ Person 1: I want you to see my A. I don't want you to see my B.

   ■ Person 2: I see your A. And I see your B. And I see so much more.

3. Round 2: Now, do the same process with:

   ■ Person 1: I want you to see my B. I don't want you to see my A.

   ■ Person 2: I see your B. And I see your A. And I see so much more.

4. Round 3: Now, go through these lines in turn:

   ■ Person 1: You will see what you will see. And I will be what I will be.

   ■ Person 2: I will see what I will see. And you will be what you will be.

5. Round 4: Now, once more taking turns, complete the statement with at least three new thoughts:

   ■ Person 1: I am pleased to offer whatever you experience of me. My acceptance allows me to … and it allows me to … and it allows me to …

   ■ Person 2: I rejoice at your acceptance. And I embrace your freedom.

23

8 Total Acceptance

Technique devised by Fran Burgess

Based on work by Steve Gilligan

I am particularly fond of this recipe as it was one of the first I ever came up with. Steve Gilligan was my muse, inspiring me by his sponsoring process. I gave it this rather grand title of Total Acceptance but it certainly takes you some way towards it!

THE INGREDIENTS

The Purpose
Suitable for developing
self-acceptance

The Conditions
Time: 20 mins
Resources: None
Who: G + E
Skill Level: Medium

The Delivery Method
Kinaesthetic: Spatial anchors

The NLP Frames
Neurological: Submodalities,
multiple perspectives
Linguistic: None

If you have already visited the Accepting Process (Recipe 7) you'll see that I have taken his original technique further. I reasoned that for many people, their source of self-imposed judgement comes from imagining what others are experiencing and thinking. It is our mind-reading that undermines us, and not what actually happened. Given that mind-reading is all about our own stuff, in truth the lack of acceptance is coming from within.

The structure here invites your Explorers to step into the shoes of their chosen witnesses and revise and update their perceptions of how they are being perceived. They will be surprised how their sternest critic can become their strongest sponsor!

As each witness circles round the space, it is as though your Explorers are building up a cauldron of ease within the emerging relational field of acceptance. This space can be quite powerful and offer some very strong insights.

20 MIN   G + E   MEDIUM

The Technique

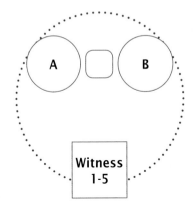

1   Select a context, either work, home, social or self. Within this context, mark out two spots:

■ To your left B – occasions when you disappoint yourself; you behave in ways that you find difficult to forgive.

■ To your right A – occasions when you are firing on all your cylinders and being magnificent.

2   Choose whichever spot you want to enter first. Step into the context and ask:

■ What are you doing, feeling and thinking?

■ Who are you when you are like this? What's important?

3   Once you have gathered this information, come out and shake it off. Make sure that you finish off on spot A, which may mean that you return to it.

4   Now identify a place opposite to you, where your selected 'audience' of five will view you. Select your sternest critic as well as your biggest fan. You can select them in advance or you can wait until you arrive at this spot.

5   Circling *outside A*, walk up to this place and meet the first one. As this witness, keeping the rhythm steady, say:

■ I see you when you are A (look at A space) and I see you when you are B (look at B space).

■ And I see you as so much more (look beyond the space between A and B).

6   Once you have a felt sense of the 'so much more', bring this person with you, *outside B* back to the start. Now select the next person, and repeat the process.

7   After all five, notice now how you are feeling – your sense of resourcefulness. Go to wherever you want to go in the space or outside of it. You can have conversations with your witnesses if you like. Absorb all the differences that have emerged.

■ How self-accepting are you feeling now? (1 low–10 high)

9 Developing Presence

Technique devised by Fran Burgess

Model devised by Leif Smith

Lara Ewing, one of the early NLP trainers in the United States, introduced this model from the work of Leif Smith, the founder of the Explorers Foundation. This very wise man lives his passion, providing opportunities to encourage everyone to go beyond their limits – to make discoveries that are there waiting to be found.

THE INGREDIENTS

The Purpose
Suitable for developing a high state of enquiry

The Conditions
Time: 20 mins
Resources: None
Who: G + E
Skill Level: Easy

The Delivery Method
Kinaesthetic: Spatial anchors

The NLP Frames
Neurological: Submodalities
Linguistic: None

He believes that explorers are 'seekers, question askers, answer listeners, conjecture framers and testers, pattern finders, song makers'. Those who know about modelling recognise a kindred spirit here. And explorers need magic.

As soon as I heard of the four ingredients of magic (wonder, integrity, sensitivity and intensity) I knew I had a new model – always a good day. Testing it out during various courses in the weeks that followed it became consistently clear that what Leif calls 'magic' I would term 'Being Present' – a state of highly attentive energy, essential for removing self-awareness and for offering full attention to the world outside of ourselves.

This is the basic state for modelling, so is well worth developing.

The Technique

1   Stand in the central space and consider an important conversation you are about to have, where you have a need to understand the other person.

- What is your level of focused energy? (1 low–10 high)

- How big, bright, moving, close, loud is the other person?

2   Step into each space and connect with a time when you experienced this state. Before you move to the next space, shake yourself so you are neutral for the next state.

- What is it feeling like?

- Where is your attention?

- What is your level of energy?

- What gesture or image emerges?

3   Now step into each space, one after the other, without a pause, and arrive in the central space. Revisit the conversation in the future.

- How big, bright, moving, close, loud is the other person now?

- What is your level of focused energy? (1 low–10 high)

4   If you want to intensify this experience then return to the different spaces and get an even more powerful description, and bring it back to the centre.

5   Identify an image, a gesture and a sound that encapsulate this state of presence. As you are reaching your optimum state, do your gesture as you hear the sound and see the image.

10 Building Excellence

Technique devised by Fran Burgess

Based on work by Jan Ardui, Rodger Bailey and Shelle Rose Charvet

I enjoyed constructing this technique, since it nicely dovetails with ideas I had been playing around with.

THE INGREDIENTS

The Purpose
Suitable for improving any performance

The Conditions
Time: 20 mins
Resources: None
Who: G + E
Skill Level: Easy

The Delivery Method
Cognitive: Relational constructs

The NLP Frames
Neurological: Time
Linguistic: Meta programmes, Temporal predicates

I had recently met up with Jan Ardui at the London NLP Conference after a gap of about 20 years. We did our trainer training together in Santa Cruz back in 1992. He has identified a concept called Generative Complementarities – opposing attributes that have to be in place to create the tension and energy required for the performance of each. Based on this thinking, he has come up with a brilliant model for Excellence, incorporating the balance between freedom and discipline and performance and alignment.

Taking one of the pairings, you need to have discipline to generate freedom – the greater the discipline, the greater the potential for freedom. However, in a bid for freedom, attention to discipline is often overridden.

I then explored both attributes in terms of their meta programme traits, à la Rodger Bailey and Shelle Rose Charvet, to identify their significant differences. And as you can see, I then mixed it around a bit to minimise the differences and generate a sense of collaboration between the two, finally topping it off with some clear evidence frame questions.

The Technique

1 Take the attributes of discipline and freedom. Think of a project that you are currently working on.

- How disciplined are you being? (1 low–10 high)

- How free are you being? (1 low–10 high)

2 To explore your thinking further, ask yourself:

- How can you bring more detail into freedom and some big picture thinking into discipline?

- How can you avoid the disadvantages of freedom whilst embracing the benefits of discipline?

- How can you apply the accrued wisdom concerning freedom whilst recognising a range of ways of being disciplined?

- How can you employ traditional approaches to applying freedom whilst introducing novel and original approaches to applying discipline?

3 Now complete these statements:

- I will know I have achieved a balance when …

- I will know I am ready to achieve more when …

- I will know I am capable of greater excellence when …

4 Consider your project once more.

- What are you going to do now?

- Looking back, when did you start?

- What were your levels of freedom and discipline then?

5 Given that there is always more to develop, for the moment you might like to continue looping around Stages 3 and 4 until you come to rest.

11 Inspiring a Task

Technique devised by Fran Burgess

Model devised by Fran Burgess and Derek Jackson

This model came to life over a bottle of red wine in a Llandudno restaurant. Derek and I were discussing those moments of great productivity when time seems to stand still or fly by, and with what seems no effort at all we are able to produce work way beyond standard. These are moments of deep satisfaction. I suspect this state is similar to the descriptions of the flow state, when sportspeople, for example, seem to perform as if possessed; where everything goes right, timing is perfect, accuracy spot on, focus sustained and energy relaxed.

THE INGREDIENTS

The Purpose
Suitable for becoming more inspired and committed to a task

The Conditions
Time: 20 mins
Resources: None
Who: G + E
Skill Level: Easy

The Delivery Method
Kinaesthetic: Spatial anchors

The NLP Frames
Neurological: None
Linguistic: Temporal predicates

In the process, we identified these four components as central to becoming inspired:

■ External stimulus: This could be a conversation, something heard on the radio or TV, or ideas found in a book or article. Whatever the source, this stimulus is needed to activate the dormant ideas.

■ Mission: You may not know what your mission is but you do know if your heart sings or sinks, or if your being rejoices or despairs. It does beg the question as to why you are doing something that doesn't enhance you and your soul.

■ Talents: This is the biblical expression for the vast reservoir of skills and knowledge gathered through your life, some not called upon for years.

■ Permission: This is an interesting one. We need to have total permission from ourselves, and from those around us, to be so self-absorbed and completely focused to the exclusion of all else. Otherwise we will talk ourselves out of total immersion.

The Technique

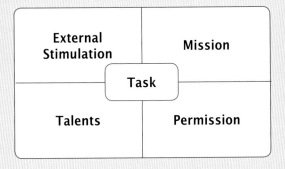

1 Identify the task. Step into the Task space.

 ■ What is your level of commitment to this task? (1 low–10 high)

2 Step into External Stimulation. Once you've answered the questions return to the Task central point and absorb your answers.

 ■ What outside information are you missing and where might it come from? (You might like to step further out.)

 ■ What have you been listening to or seeing recently that could now be connected to your task?

3 Step into Mission and reconnect with your sense of purpose – what is *really* important to you. Answer the questions then return to the Task space.

 ■ How is this task contributing directly or indirectly to your mission and your sense of purpose?

 ■ How might you alter this task, or the way you are doing it, so that it becomes more aligned to who you are and all that honours you?

4 Step into your Talents, gathered throughout your entire life. Answer the questions then return to the Task space.

 ■ How might you use this task to use your talents even more?

 ■ Which of your talents could you be bringing to this task that you haven't thought of yet? What might others suggest?

5 Step into Permission and be aware of who might have something to say about you and your task. Answer the questions then return to the Task space.

 ■ Given the time you need to devote solely to this task, is this OK with everyone around you, including yourself?

 ■ How might you get around any objections?

6 Return to the Task space.

 ■ What is your level of commitment to the task now? (1 low–10 high)

7 If there has been insufficient shift, you may choose to revisit any of the spaces for further information.

12 Modelling Your Anxiety

Technique devised by Fran Burgess

Model devised by Paul Salkovskis

Paul Salkovskis, Professor of Clinical Psychology and Applied Science and Clinical Director of the Maudsley Hospital Centre for Anxiety Disorders and Trauma, came up with this equation to demonstrate the dynamic of anxiety. He suggests that anxiety results from the combination of:

- Probability: the likelihood of something 'bad' happening

- Consequences: the impact of this happening

- Coping: the ability to cope with the eventualities

- Rescue: the possibility of being saved from the dire consequences

My psychotherapy supervisor, Malcolm Bray, introduced me to this model and, as ever, when gifted with a model, I sought ways of NLP-ising it and came up with a floor plan that forms the basis for this recipe.

By reversing the 1–10 scales for Coping and Rescue I have accommodated Salkovskis's equation, where levels of Coping and Rescue are divided into the sum of the levels of Probability and Consequences. Given that within NLP, we seek to be at cause, I have turned Rescue into Resources, which are under our control.

This technique is a godsend. It offers your Explorers a fabulous route to regaining control over their worlds and the sources of their anxiety; in fact, it is the belief that they don't have control that triggers this constricting state in the first place. This recipe seeks to redress that balance.

THE INGREDIENTS

The Purpose
Suitable for managing anxiety

The Conditions
Time: 20 mins
Resources: None
Who: G + E
Skill Level: Advanced

The Delivery Method
Kinaesthetic: Spatial anchors, sliding scales

The NLP Frames
Neurological: None
Linguistic: Temporal predicates

20 MIN   G + E   ADVANCED

The Technique

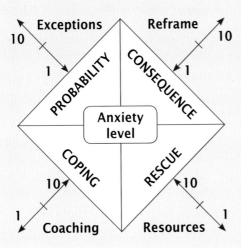

Notice that the bottom two go from 10 (low) to 1 (high) and not the other way round. This isn't a typo!

1 Consider the event that is causing the anxiety.

■ What is your level of anxiety ? (1 high–10 low)

2 Stand in the centre of the diamond. For each aspect, hear its question and then begin to walk along the arm until your feet naturally stop – to match the intensity of your response to the question. Record the point of the scale you reach and your answers.

■ Probability: How likely is it that this event is going to happen the way you imagine?

■ Consequence: How strong do you think the impact of such an outcome would be?

■ Coping: How confident are you of your ability to manage these outcomes?

■ Rescue: How available are resources and support?

3 Return to the centre and once more face each of the four arms in turn. Answer the question, and take yourself to where you are now on the arm. Record your answers.

■ Exceptions: When hasn't this happened, particularly when it was expected? When else? When did it happen in a reduced way (duration, frequency, severity)?

■ Reframing: What else could happen instead? What might others expect to happen? How might others interpret these outcomes?

■ Coaching: How have you managed similar situations in the past? What are you really good at, and how useful would these skills be here and now? What could you do more of/less of that would make a difference?

■ Resourcing: What advice can you call upon at this moment? What resources have you overlooked which could be helpful here? What would someone else find to do?

4 Now, standing in the centre, consider your sense of inevitability, your certainty, your self-confidence and your levels of support.

■ What is your level of anxiety? (1 high–10 low)

13 Anxiety Animal Magic

Technique devised by Fran Burgess

Original model devised by Paul Salkovskis

This is another recipe based on the work of Paul Salkovskis from the Maudsley Hospital Centre for Anxiety Disorders and Trauma. Following on from Modelling Anxiety (Recipe 12), this is another technique to help you learn more about how you build up your state of anxiety.

THE INGREDIENTS

The Purpose
Suitable for managing anxiety

The Conditions
Time: 20 mins
Resources: None
Who: G + E
Skill Level: Easy

The Delivery Method
Kinaesthetic: Spatial anchors

The NLP Frames
Neurological: Multiple perspectives, time, metaphor
Linguistic: None

It works on the basis that there are times when you are not anxious – when you are more than equal to the situation you find yourself in – so you must have an inner mechanism that can help you to self-regulate anxiety. This technique brings this fine strategy to the surface and rewards you with hope for future times when you can discover that you are bigger than 'it'.

20 MIN   G + E   EASY

The Technique

The event

Past ◄————————————► Future

Present

1   Consider an event in the future that could cause you anxiety. As you think about it now:

   ■   What is your level of anxiety?
      (1 low–10 high)

2   Imagine a line in front of you that represents your past, present and future.

3   Walk alongside it, towards the past, until you arrive at a point when you were really anxious at a much younger age. Go back as far as you like. As you look onto this event:

   ■   What is happening?

   ■   If you were an animal, what kind of animal are you being? What sort of animal would be much more useful?

You may choose a range of different animals, to see which one suits the best.

   ■   How is this new animal responding to the source of anxiety? What does it know, believe, feel?

4   Once you are *really* clear about how this new animal behaves, step onto the line, into the event, and take on the energy of your new animal.

   ■   How are you now responding? What do you believe?

If this doesn't feel right for you, then choose another animal that works better.

   ■   What do you say to yourself, to those involved and to the anxiety itself?

   ■   Notice your level of control and how significant you feel.

5   Travel even further back.

   ■   What animal can you be when you are not anxious? What does this animal believe and know about anxiety?

6   Bringing both animals with you, walk up to the present, drawing on your animal magic should you need to. Do this several times, until you are free of any residual anxious emotions.

7   Now walk into the event that is coming up.

   ■   How are your animals responding?

   ■   What is your level of anxiety?
      (1 low–10 high)

8   Walk into this future event and experience what it is like with much less anxiety. Notice what you are doing, feeling and thinking. What are others seeing, hearing and feeling?

Establish that the anxiety level is fully acceptable before you move onto the final stage. If it isn't, go back to reinforce it further.

14 The A (Anxiety) Team

Technique devised by Fran Burgess

Model devised by Paul Salkovskis

Here is yet another treatment of the Paul Salkovskis's Anxiety Model, details of which you'll find in the previous two recipes (12 and 13). I have taken the components and turned these into archetypal energies, or more specifically Parts. This way you can work with the interactions between states held by these supporting parts.

THE INGREDIENTS

The Purpose
Suitable for managing anxiety

The Conditions
Time: 30 mins
Resources: None
Who: G + E
Skill Level: Medium

The Delivery Method
Cognitive: Questions

The NLP Frames
Neurological: Parts
Linguistic: Meta Model

Parts are a metaphorical way of representing different aspects of our personality. Acting as if they are individual 'munchkins' in their own right, enables us to call an emergency meeting and draw upon their respective knowledge and skills in support of a particular issue.

For this process, you'll see the connection between the original components and the identified parts. I have assumed there is an Emotional part, which experiences anxiety; a Coping part, in charge of getting on and doing; a Procurer part, responsible for gathering whatever resources are needed; a Rational part, bringing together information and solving problems; and an Archivist part, recording your memories and history.

Working from Salkovskis's model, you can use the natural resources that are already within your Explorers and use their existing wisdom to generate new responses to old anxiety-inducing situations.

I have opted for a purely cognitive approach, which is great if you don't have much space, are short of time or if this suits your Explorer best. You could, of course, create five spaces on the floor for each of the parts with the emotional part in the centre receiving the answers.

30 MIN   G + E   MEDIUM

The Technique

1 Consider an event that is causing you anxiety.

■ What is your level of anxiety? (1 low–10 high)

2 Invite the Emotional part to come forward and thank it for alerting you to this stressful event. Let it know that he or she will shortly have a strong team to support and protect you.

3 Call on your Coping part, your Procurer part, your Rational part and your Archivist part, and become aware of what each of them looks like. If any are very young, then fast forward them and bring them up to an age most suited to their job. Conversely, if any are much older, then they might appreciate a younger pair of legs. You want to feel that you have a solid team!

4 Ask each of them the following questions and, if you wish, record your answers to refer to later.

5 Check in with the Emotional part and ask him or her if this is sufficient to remove the anxiety response.

■ What else does any one or all of them need to do?

■ Is there anything else that needs to happen?

6 Continue the dialogue until the Emotional part is comfortable and feels the team is in place to support him or her. As you consider this event:

■ What is your level of anxiety? (1 low–10 high)

	What do you think the Emotional part needs to know? Needs to have?	What do you think the Emotional part wants to know? Wants to have?	What do you have to do now to support the Emotional part?
Coping part			
Procurer part			
Rational part			
Archivist part			

15 Balance of Power

Model and technique devised by Fran Burgess

For many years I have been playing around with the notions of power and control, and their complementarities, safety and vulnerability. They seemed not only to inform my own behaviours and decision-making but also those of my clients. This could of course be projection, but I don't think so.

THE INGREDIENTS

The Purpose
Suitable for creating personal effectiveness

The Conditions
Time: 30–40 mins
Resources: None
Who: G + E
Skill Level: Advanced

The Delivery Method
Kinaesthetic: Spatial anchors

The NLP Frames
Neurological: Submodalities
Linguistic: None

Putting the four elements together has created an extraordinarily fertile exploration ground for strengthening personal effectiveness and resolve.

Each element has its own polarities, neither of which is desirable in their extremes. Ideally our optimum operating area is ± 2.5.

■ Control: Being over-controlling can be as counterproductive as having no control at all.

■ Power: Being over-powering can be as damaging as having no sense of personal power.

■ Safety: Being cocooned in safety inhibits action just as strongly as feeling very unsafe.

■ Vulnerability: Being protective is as unproductive as feeling fully exposed.

This recipe allows your Explorers to explore, choosing different contexts, the desirable levels needed to generate their own sense of self-effectiveness. You also can detect where their coping practices have caused them to develop over-dependence. Once realised, adjustments can be made creating a more balanced system.

30-40 MIN   G + E   ADVANCED

The Technique

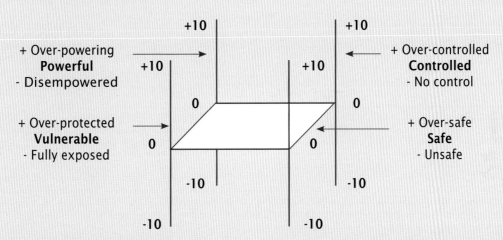

1 Consider a situation you are experiencing at the moment where you are feeling uncertain, tentative, diminished, fearful or unresourceful.

   ■ How strong is your sense of personal effectiveness? (1 low–10 high)

2 Create a square with Power, Vulnerability, Safety and Control at each corner. Each has a high 0–+10 and low 0–-10 level description. Stand in each space and determine where you are on each.

   ■ What would have to happen for the rating to reduce or increase?

   ■ How much would be too much or too little?

   Your Explorer may find that some states are more extreme than others.

3 From one corner, look at the other three corners in turn.

   ■ What do you notice about the size, shape, colour and sound of each of them? What would have to happen to make them the same?

   ■ What happens when you change them?

   Your Explorer may want to move independently around the space to gather more information.

   If there is a reluctance to move into a particular space, then you can use a metaphor to remove the blockage

   ■ How are they connected to each other? How strong or weak is this connection?

39

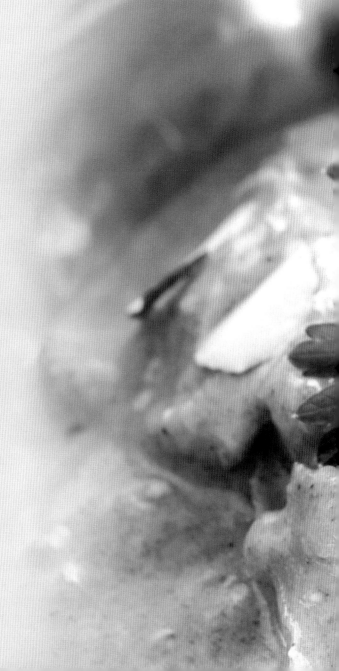

4   Stand in the centre and notice the sense of balance you have.

- ■ Are the corners equally distant from you? What happens when you bring them in or move them further out?

- ■ Are you the same size in each of them, or larger or smaller? What happens if you adjust them so that you are life size in each?

5   Make whatever adjustments you wish to make. Ideally you want to be within -2 to +2 for each element. Then stand in the middle and ask yourself:

- ■ How personally effective are you feeling now? (1 low–10 high)

16 A Powerful Story

Model and technique devised by Fran Burgess

Here is another way to work with the four elements of power, control, vulnerability and safety, which I believe are the ingredients that directly influence our sense of wellbeing and self-assurance and our ability to go forward into the world. Time and again with my therapy clients, and certainly with learners, one or other of these elements prove to be the cause of stuckness and the inability to achieve goals. It is about our fear of being vulnerable and unsafe, and coping through fighting the wrong battles and not letting go.

THE INGREDIENTS

The Purpose
Suitable for strengthening personal effectiveness

The Conditions
Time: 20 mins
Resources: None
Who: E group
Skill Level: Easy

The Delivery Method
Auditory: A story

The NLP Frames
Neurological: Multiple perspectives,
Linguistic: None

Of course, since this has been my own personal journey over the years, it might be that I am just projecting my own stuff onto others. However, I have been fairly rigorous about testing my perceptions, so I feel that I can be equal to that particular accusation. In fact, when I offer this model to clients, it comes as a relief to many to finally have a way of thinking about their own situation and a means to identify what they can do to make a difference.

To ring the changes, I have opted to go for a metaphorical story, translating the elements into key archetypes and working with the focus and fears of each.

- ■ Power = King
- ■ Control = Guards
- ■ Vulnerability = Nurse
- ■ Safety = Child

I hope you enjoy the story. You can choose to read it out to the full group, record it and offer it on CD or MP3, or give your Explorer the script to read themselves. Make sure you honour your sources.

The Technique

Once upon a time, long long ago, in a land far away, a child, who happened to be a prince, awoke from a bad dream, crying and calling out for his ever-attentive nurse. As usual, she came rushing in and immediately calmed and reassured him that all would be well; that the bogeymen would be banished and he would be safe forever. She tucked him in and with more soothing words kissed him on the forehead and bade him go back to sleep. She returned to her bed by the door, always making sure that he would be safe.

The boy's father came to hear about his son's nightmares and about the dark riders who were invading his dreams. His father, who understood that many an important message came in dreams, feared that this might be an omen of ill portent. Being a strong ruler, he knew that he ought to act swiftly, so decreed that all persons dressed in black should be seized and locked up in the deepest dungeons. He brought together his court guards, led by his most trusted warrior, and instructed them to be on full alert, ever watchful of any suspicious event or cause for concern which might bring harm upon his child. His sent out word that everyone should be on their guard and report back the first signs of danger. Soon the whole kingdom was watchful, mindful of the need to keep the prince safe and protected.

After a long while, the prince became bored and frustrated. He wasn't allowed to go out to play on his own. He wasn't allowed to venture into the furthermost corners of the castle without his nurse or the guards being with him. His father the king would daily enquire after his wellbeing, and became clearly fretful if his son didn't offer chapter and verse his peace of mind. He languished in his nursery starved of new experiences and stimulation. Even worse, he soon began to believe what the others were saying, jumping at his own shadow and imagining terrible goings on just behind the walls.

The whole castle and kingdom became more and more anxious lest the young prince waste totally away. A national emergency was about to be declared, since by now the young prince refused to eat, and cried often and long in his bedchamber.

Then, at the darkest hour, a soothsayer appeared, well versed in what had come to pass.

'Nurse!' he cried. 'You will harm the boy more by your caring than you ever will by your courage to let him explore and fend for himself.' 'Guard!' he cried. 'Peace will spread throughout the land when you lessen your grip and allow strength to grow of its own accord.' 'Oh King!' he cried. 'Your wisdom knows the power that comes from within has far more longevity than any power that is imposed. Resilience comes from overcoming fear.'

And since everyone listened to what the soothsayer had to say, the nurse stopped being so protective, the guard stopped being so controlling and the king stopped being so over-powering. To everyone's amazement, in an instant the young prince reclaimed his energy. He became bolder and more courageous, but not wilful and wanton. He began to relish challenges, knowing that he had other people to fall back on. When he needed help, he asked for it, but not before he had tried to find out a way for himself. His dreams were now full of adventure and daring deeds.

As the moons passed over the night skies, the prince was soon a young man of great stature and renown. His nurse and his guard were still in attendance should he need them.

His father the king stood back delighting in his son's independence.

Eventually word spread throughout the land that all was safe and everyone breathed a huge sigh of relief. They found they could relax and go about their day-to-day activities with a lighter step and a gladder heart. Laughter and ease began to spread throughout the kingdom and all began to believe that the world was indeed a place that they were equal to.

The kingdom began to be known as a land of welcome, adventure and fun, open to greeting and learning from the many travellers who were drawn to their hearths, listening with wonder to the tales of worlds beyond the mountains.

And for some, this was an invitation to travel further afield themselves, knowing with confidence that they were protected by their own wisdom, freedom, calm and compassion.

Task

You may have identified with one of the characters in this story more than the others. Or you may be more aware of a particular relationship between two of them.

Start a series of correspondence between you and your chosen character. Begin by writing to the character and then writing their reply in return. You can continue these letters until they provide you with no further useful information or insight.

I do advise that you do the letter-writing. Imaginary conversations alone can go some way in exploring your feelings, but you will be surprised by just how much more you get from deliberately putting pen to paper.

17 Stuff Happens (Part 1)

Model and technique devised by Fran Burgess

I created this model whilst working with a client who was suffering from stress verging on depression. He had fairly recently arrived to head up a division and his was a story of juggling and plate-spinning, working long hours and constantly being available on the phone, poised to fire-fight. He gave three recent events at work that culminated in him booking the session.

THE INGREDIENTS

The Purpose
Suitable for strengthening personal empowerment

The Conditions
Time: 40 mins
Resources: None
Who: G + E
Skill Level: Medium

The Delivery Method
Kinaesthetic: Spatial anchors, somatic syntax
Cognitive: Relational constructs

The NLP Frames
Neurological: Submodalities, metaphor
Linguistic: Meta Model

I could feel his tension and stress. It was so important to him that people thought well of him. If things went wrong, then others might find out that he couldn't cope, which would have been the ultimate hell for him.

I wanted him to realise that he did have resources he could draw upon, that he was not totally dependent on the goodwill and blind eye of others, and that he could trust himself much more than he would have given himself credit for.

I created what became the Stuff Happens model, borrowing a bit from Transactional Analysis and Eric Berne's OK Corral, and set up my own Cartesian coordinates. My client was able to gain resources to manage not just his work situation, but his social life as well. Then, as I used the model more and more with other clients experiencing stress and anxiety, a highly effective process began to emerge.

I have split it into two parts, since the second part requires a high level of skill to manage the process and keep the Explorer safe and steady in the process of exploration. You need to consider the ecology of going deeper with your Explorer if it takes you beyond your skill level.

40 MIN G + E MEDIUM

The Technique

1. Stuff happens and I'm OK	3. Stuff mustn't happen and I'm OK
2. Stuff happens and I'm not OK	4. Stuff mustn't happen and I'm not OK

This process helps you deal with levels of anxiety you may be running in particular situations, whether at home, at work or with friends.

1 Each square holds a different experience:

> Read the descriptions of the squares so that your Explorer has a clear sense of each.

- Square 1: Things are going wrong and you have some responsibility for it but it doesn't affect you. You stay undiminished.

- Square 2: Balls and spinning plates are dropping. With each one you feel worse since you are responsible.

- Square 3: You are managing to prevent things going wrong and are able to keep things under control.

- Square 4: You are unable to prevent things going wrong and you have no control.

> Your Explorer may not want to stay too long in this space, so just get the needed information then come out and shake it off as soon as possible.

2 Walk into each space and access a time when such events occurred.

- What gesture or posture sums up your feelings?

- What symbol comes to mind?

- What are the size, colour and sounds associated with this space?

3 Now practise going from Square 2 to Square 1, from Square 3 to Square 1, then from Square 4 to Square 1. For Square 4, you may choose to go directly or via Squares 2 or 3. At the point of crossing the line into Square 1, breathe, change into Square 1 posture or movement and say to yourself:

- Stuff happens and I'm OK.

4 Keep doing this until you are confident that whatever happens, you can quickly access the sanctuary of Square 1.

- What are you now noticing about the size, shape and colour of the various squares?

- What are you now telling yourself?

5 Now choose a work, social, family or relationship context. Once more, step into each of the squares and notice any occasions that arise which may match that square. Test out your ability to move easily to Square 1.

18 Stuff Happens (Part 2)

Model and technique devised by Fran Burgess

Following on from Part 1 of this technique (Recipe 17), Part 2 takes the Explorer deeper into the internal structure of what is going on.

THE INGREDIENTS

The Purpose
Suitable for redesigning the rules we live by

The Conditions
Time: 45 mins
Resources: None
Who: G + E
Skill Level: Advanced

The Delivery Method
Kinaesthetic: Spatial anchors
Cognitive: Questions

The NLP Frames
Neurological: Submodalities, metaphor
Linguistic: Meta Model

I find that for most Explorers who have issues about anxiety and performance, Square 3 produces real tension. Here they never drop their guard, they are fully alert and firing on all cylinders, and they are being equal to all that is thrown at them – until they can withstand the pressure no longer and the spinning plates begin to fall. As I see it, this is the land of coping, symbolised by clenched teeth and white knuckles. Wellbeing is dependent on the approval of others, while survival relies on giving them what they want to avoid being found out.

These Explorers are living by the rules of others and tick all the boxes when it comes to the five basic drivers of transactional analysis:

- Be strong
- Hurry up
- Be perfect
- Please others
- Try hard

We learn these instructions at an early age and seek not to disappoint. However, we may find that these very instructions become the tail that wags our dog.

This technique seeks to help Explorers regain a sense of personal control and self-determination. *They* can decide the rules that govern the injunctions about what must or mustn't happen.

When I'm the guide I like to stand by Square 4, so that I can sponsor the Explorer and give him or her firm support just by being there, congruently and lovingly.

The Technique

1. Stuff happens and I'm OK

3. Stuff mustn't happen and I'm OK

2. Stuff happens and I'm not OK

4. Stuff mustn't happen and I'm not OK

1   Following on from Part 1, go to Square 3. With each of the drivers record your answers to the following questions, so that you learn why you work so hard to be in control. You will discover how others have been setting your agenda. Take the *opposite* of the driver, so that you are able to discover the consequences of failing:

- Be strong becomes Being weak

- Hurry up becomes Taking too much time

- Be Perfect becomes Failing and making mistakes

- Please Others becomes Pleasing yourself or not pleasing others

- Try harder becomes Not trying hard enough

2   For each driver, record your answers to the following statements:

> Read out the questions and record the answers.

- Being [the opposite of the driver] leads to …

- People who are [the opposite of the driver] are … which means …

- If I am [the opposite of the driver], people will think I am …

3   Step into Square 4. Allow whatever memories to emerge.

Watch out! This could be an uncomfortable place for your Explorer.

4   In this space, despite what might be happening, become aware of your inner power and where it is inside of you.

   ■ What shape is it, colour, texture and temperature?

   ■ What is it like? Does a metaphor come to mind?

5   Let this inner power grow and grow, until you are much bigger, much stronger and so much more than you were then.

6   Step back to Square 3, bringing this power with you. There are many important personal values that you mustn't violate, of course, with being true to yourself a major one, so you want to ensure that you are able to protect what really is important to you. You are now in charge of the agenda.

   ■ What personal values are really important to you?

   ■ What would you do to live up to them?

7   Your personal charter: list those behaviours that demonstrate what is deeply important to you.

8   Now return to the list of your recorded answers.

Read back the earlier answers.

   ■ What is your response now to those questions?

19 It's the Way You See 'Em

Technique source unknown

Based on work by Richard Bandler

I came to the awareness that I had something called *internal representations* fairly late in life. I was in my mid-thirties before I realised I was creating spontaneous, unbidden mental images in my mind to accompany what was happening in the 'real' world. I may have been aware of the voices inside my head, which I called 'hearing myself think'. I was aware of the different emotions I was feeling, but possibly I was not tuned in to the subtle shifts and distinctions between one and another.

THE INGREDIENTS

The Purpose
Suitable for improving any performance

The Conditions
Time: 20 mins
Resources: None
Who: G + E
Skill Level: Easy

The Delivery Method
Cognitive: Questions

The NLP Frames
Neurological: Submodalities
Linguistic: None

Until I was introduced to NLP it would never have crossed my mind to describe the structure of these images, sounds or feelings. Richard Bandler is credited with giving us the language to describe the construction of these internal processes. This amazing piece of modelling therefore offers us the opportunity to restructure our construction, and so create the opportunity to build a completely different response.

I've used this reconstruction process to work on a performance that you are unhappy with, although this contrastive analysis process can also be used with beliefs, skills and relationships.

The Technique

1. Think of a situation where you performed poorly which you want to improve.

   ■ How would you rate your performance? (1 low–10 high)

2. As if looking at a screen above eye level, see yourself in this situation. Looking at this image notice:

   ■ What size is the picture? Where is it?

   ■ How bright is it? How colourful?

   ■ Is it focused or blurry?

   ■ Is it moving like a film or still like a photograph?

   ■ Is it framed or unframed?

   ■ Is it in 2D or 3D?

   ■ Are you life-size, larger than life or smaller than life?

   ■ Are you in the picture or looking at yourself?

   Write down the answers, so that you can compare with the next set of answers

3. Move this image to one side. Now select a situation where your performance really pleases you. Place this image on the screen and go through the same process.

   ■ How does this one differ from the first?

4. Return to the first image. Reconstruct it so that it looks like the second image. If the second one was in colour and the first was black and white, then change the first one to colour. Make the adjustments so that you feel much better when you look at it.

5. Once the image of the first situation is to your liking, step into the picture and experience the situation now through your eyes and ears.

   ■ Notice the differences.

   ■ How would you rate your performance? (1 low–10 high)

   If there is not enough improvement either suggest a different 'good' performance or go back to Step 4 and increase the degree of change being made.

53

20 Strengthening Performance

Model and technique devised by John McWhirter

I have used John McWhirter's hierarchical model Performance, Management, Direction many times, either standalone or as part of an overall process. I find that it never lets me down and always provides critical information for the Explorer.

THE INGREDIENTS

The Purpose
Suitable for developing and finely tuning a performance

The Conditions
Time: 20 mins
Resources: None
Who: G + E
Skill Level: Easy

The Delivery Method
Kinaesthetic: Spatial anchors
Cognitive: Questions

The NLP Frames
Neurological: None
Linguistic: None

Its strength is in its simplicity. Based on John's fundamental What, How, Why, thinking, this is a tremendous model for coaches to diagnose the source of any weakness in performance, and therefore identify where attention can most usefully be placed. I like it because it gives great autonomy to the Explorer, whose internal wisdom can drive the improvement process.

It is particularly versatile. You can apply this model to all levels of performance – operational, management or strategic. You can apply it to individuals, groups, organisations and cultures.

I've opted to provide it unembellished, just how John first introduced it many years ago.

The Technique

Direction

Supervision Management

Performance

1 Select a performance you want to improve. Be clear of the context in which you will be performing.

■ What is your level of current performance? (1 low–10 high)

■ What level do you want to achieve at this stage?

2 Performance: Step into this space facing the context.

■ What are you doing? What else?

■ What are you not doing that you could be doing?

■ What is important to you here?

3 Management: Step back into this space still facing the context.

■ How do you know what to do when?

■ How do you know which options to choose?

■ How do you evaluate the feedback you're getting?

4 Direction: Step back into this space still facing the context.

■ Why do you choose to do these things?

■ Why did you arrive at this thinking?

■ Why is all of this important?

5 Supervision: Step to the side and pay attention to each of these spaces.

■ What are you noticing?

■ What suggestions do you need to make?

■ What additional awareness is required?

6 Working your way from Direction back down to Performance, explore the suggestions coming from Supervision and make your adjustments as required. Finally, stepping into your context:

■ What is your level of performance now? (1 low–10 high)

21 Getting Better

Technique devised by Fran Burgess

This simple technique has all the hallmarks of NLP thinking, and proves to be a really useful addition to any coach's repertoire.

THE INGREDIENTS

The Purpose
Suitable for developing an ability

The Conditions
Time: 15 mins
Resources: None
Who: G + E
Skill Level: Easy

The Delivery Method
Kinaesthetic: Spatial anchors
Cognitive: Questions

The NLP Frames
Neurological: Anchoring neurological levels
Linguistic: Meta Model, temporal predicates

It draws on the NLP presupposition that we have all the resources we need already. It calls upon self-modelling to find out and draw upon what already works, based on the higher neurological levels of beliefs, values and identity. It directs attention through language using our trusty Meta Model patterns, time distortion with a sprinkling of temporal predicates and some presuppositional stances thrown in for good measure.

Fundamentally it draws on the merging of resources, using what works to inspire what doesn't work – yet – through a process of stacking anchors. I have to say I felt delightfully pleased as it emerged.

However, if that is all gobbledegook to you, no worries, since it is just a pleasant process to do. Knowing the technical thinking behind it doesn't make it work any better.

I have opted to give it a spatial anchor treatment, though I suspect it could be equally effective using your left hand for current ability and right hand for desired ability, bringing the left hand over to the right hand to 'donate' the information.

The Technique

1   Set out two spaces on the floor – your current ability on the left and your desired ability on the right.

2   Have your partner record your answers as you move backwards and forwards between the two spaces.

I am good at X.	I want to be better at Y. My commitment to doing Y is … (1 low–10 high)

When I do X I feel …	When I do Y I feel …
When I do X I tell myself …	When I do Y I tell myself …
When I do X I know …	When I do Y I know …
X is important because …	Y is important because …
With X I am like …	With Y I am like …
When I was getting better at X, I thought …	Now I am getting better at Y, I think …
Getting better at X leads me to …	Getting better at Y leads me to …
Becoming good at X led to …	Becoming good at Y has led to …
Being good at X means …	Being good at Y means …
What is your commitment now to doing Y? (1 low–10 high)	
What is the first thing you are going to do now?	

22 Managing Wellbeing

Model and technique devised by Fran Burgess

I came across something called the Network Management Model, created by the International Organization for Standardization under the direction of Open Systems Interconnection. The Network Management Model seeks to maintain IT networks and safeguard trouble-free operations through monitoring faults, changes, uptake, performance and security.

THE INGREDIENTS

The Purpose
Suitable for developing and
finely tuning a performance

The Conditions
Time: 20 mins
Resources: None
Who: G + E
Skill Level: Easy

The Delivery Method
Cognitive: Questions

The NLP Frames
Neurological: None
Linguistic: Meta Model

How wonderful it would be if we could achieve that in life, I thought! Wouldn't it be great to have a way of making sure our major decisions are going to take us where we want to be? How often is our own wellbeing affected by our anxiety and concerns that we are not in control of where we are going?

This got me to thinking. With slight modifications I have come up with an indicator to diagnose and evaluate our levels of overall wellbeing – a bit of an emotional MOT! I hope you find this really useful. If it works as a model then it should help us to navigate through a system and alert us to where the problems lie.

The Technique

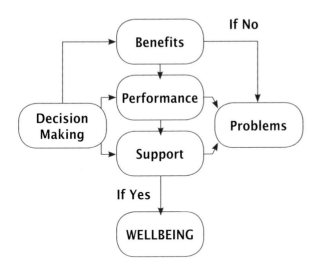

Benefits

Performance

Decision Making

Problems

Support

If No

If Yes

WELLBEING

1. If you are going for the full MOT you will want to go through each area in your life – work, home and social. Or you may just want to zone in on a particular issue.

   ■ What is your level of wellbeing in this area? (1 low–10 high)

2. List the significant decisions you have taken which have had a direct influence on this area of your life. Against each of them work through the following framework of questions:

   ■ Are you reaping all the intended benefits of this decision? How frequently do you appreciate the benefits you have gained?

   ■ Is this decision worth the resources it cost – time, emotion, energy, money? Is this decision still relevant? Will this decision hold for another 12 months?

   ■ Does this decision involve the right people and resources? Have you been getting the right quality of support to sustain this decision? Does this decision keep you sufficiently protected from 'toxic' influences?

3. If you have answered no to any one of these, then consider that this factor may be contributing to possible problems you are experiencing or any sense of dissatisfaction.

4. Isolate your no answers and set yourself the task of making new decisions to eliminate these effects.

   ■ What do I now have to pay attention to and consider?

   ■ What does this situation call for?

   ■ What is now required so that the benefits are forthcoming, within available resources, given the prevailing conditions?

5. Imagine being in this position 12 months from now.

   ■ From this position in the future, have these new decisions raised your level of wellbeing to the level you desire?

23 Space Cadet

Technique devised by Fran Burgess

Based on work by John McWhirter

This process shines with simplicity. In this instance I have chosen to work with an unuseful belief, one which doesn't support you in your chosen goals. You could instead use a situation or a state.

THE INGREDIENTS

The Purpose
Suitable for loosening your grip on an unsupportive belief

The Conditions
Time: 10 mins
Resources: None
Who: G + E
Skill Level: Easy

The Delivery Method
Cognitive: Questions

The NLP Frames
Neurological: None
Linguistic: Spatial predicates

Working on the understanding that each of us constructs our experiences in our own unique way, it is more useful to work with this construction and not take up time focusing on the details of the story. So here we are looking literally at the spatial nature of the construction – where the construction is located and where we are in relation to it.

When I worked through this exercise myself (ideally I could have done with someone reading the questions to me), I was amazed at how my thinking shifted depending on where I was thinking from. I hadn't even realised that I was thinking from a particular physical location in the first place, and that was contributing to my stuckness!

The Technique

You can encourage your Explorer to stand up and move around to make the exercise come alive even more.

1 Think of something you believe about yourself which you know limits you and holds you back. Or maybe you would like to choose a belief that you want to strengthen.

- How strongly do you believe this? (1 low–10 high)

2 Pay attention to:

- Where do you hold this belief in your body?

- What size and shape is it?

3 Now, with this awareness, notice what happens when you place yourself:

- Inside this belief. Way inside this belief.

- Above this belief. High above this belief.

- Beneath this belief. Way below this belief.

- Alongside this belief. Close to this belief. Parallel to this belief.

- Behind this belief. Far behind this belief.

- In front of this belief. Way in front of this belief.

4 Notice which particular position(s) had the greatest impact on you in reducing your certainty about this belief, or increasing your commitment to relate more positively to this belief.

- What can you now do to serve you in relation to this belief?

- What has happened to the size and shape of the belief?

- How strongly do you believe this? (1 low–10 high)

24 Time Traveller

Technique devised by Fran Burgess

Involving work developed by Robert Dilts

This process begins to dig into the ins and outs of your belief system, and gets to the heartland of NLP linguistic practices. It is delightful as a means of working with a pesky belief that is limiting your Explorers' lives in a way that is kind to their system and respectful to how the beliefs were originally formed.

THE INGREDIENTS

The Purpose
Suitable for loosening your grip on an unsupportive belief

The Conditions
Time: 10 mins
Resources: None
Who: G + E
Skill Level: Easy

The Delivery Method
Cognitive: Questions

The NLP Frames
Neurological: Time
Linguistic: Temporal predicates, Meta Model

It works on loosening the certainty they hold about the belief – rather like working free a baby tooth for the tooth fairy magically to take away in the middle of the night. Bizarrely, by changing the tenses of verbs they use, you can rock them backwards and forwards in time, allowing them to slip slithers of new thinking into the chinks this provides. Apologies for the mixing of metaphors here!

I would advise that with this one your Explorers work on their own, and write down their answers. They may be keeping a journal – a really useful resource particularly if they are going through a period of change – and in this way they can keep a record to refer back to later on. It is great to have real live evidence of how much they have changed.

However, my testers also reported that it was good to have someone asking the questions, which left the Explorer time just to explore. This is great, provided you leave the Explorer free to go where he or she needs to go, without comment or interruption.

Technically the language construction combines the use of temporal predicates with Aristotle's thinking which was codified by Robert Dilts. For more about this, check out the fantastic NLP Encyclopedia at www.nlpu.com.

The Technique

1. Think of something you believe about yourself which you know limits you and holds you back.

   - How strongly do you believe this? (1 low–10 high)

2. Pay attention to:

   - Where do you hold this belief in your body?

   - What size and shape is it?

3. Now, with this awareness, complete the following sentences.

   - I have this belief because …

   - I still have this belief which means …

   - Having this belief leads to …

   - I will have had this belief so long as …

   - I would have that belief if …

   - I used to have that belief since …

   - I have had that belief until …

   - Having had that belief I can now …

   - People who let go of such a belief are therefore …

4. Return to the original belief.

   - What has happened to the size and shape of the belief?

   - How strongly do you believe this? (1 low–10 high)

25 Who Am I?

Model and technique devised by Fran Burgess

Modelling is at the heart of NLP. It is the process of taking live experiences and, through a series of stages, turning this into a simple construction. Easier said than done!

THE INGREDIENTS

The Purpose
Suitable for strengthening identity

The Conditions
Time: 45 mins
Resources: Cards, scissors, photocopier
Who: E
Skill Level: Easy

The Delivery Method
Cognitive: Card sort

The NLP Frames
Neurological: None
Linguistic: None

The Modelling Process Model is a sequential model itself, and one that does require the development of skills and awareness. Within NLP we have many questioning frameworks to gather verbal information as well as our sensory acuity to notice non-verbals. However, many people come to a halt at this stage, not knowing what to do with all the data they have gathered

This technique helps us practise and develop our capacity to sort through data and flex up our ability to detect patterns. It can be applied to self-modelling and modelling another person, situation or relationship. You are spoilt for choice.

Using a list of adjectives to act as our data, and tipping my cap to the Johari window, I have come up with a card sort approach which provides an external illustration of internal sorting processes. With these, your Explorers can discover the different permutations that can emerge. For best learning, ask two or three Explorers to work parallel to each other. This way they will gain direct evidence of the differences between individuals.

The data for this card sort is found in Appendix 1. Photocopy these so that you have a complete set for the number of people involved, possibly on different coloured paper for each set. Make sure you collate them before you cut them up, or else you will get into a right mess! Similarly, make sure your Explorers don't mix them up with other sets, so have a few extra paper clips or elastic bands to hand.

45 MIN   EASY

The Technique

1 Here is a selection of topics to model. Select just one of them at a time If you do more than three in total you will give yourself the chance to notice possible patterns.

- A role

- A colleague, friend, partner

- A relationship

- An organisation

Sorting process

2 You can choose to work only with positive attributes to highlight 'what is there' or with negative qualities as well to balance this with 'what isn't there'. Going with both will give you a richer picture. Set up three columns.

Definitely Applicable	Applicable	Not Applicable

3 Select one relationship and sort the cards under these categories. Go with your gut response. Ask:

- Does this attribute apply to me as I relate with this person/role/relationship/organisation?

Pattern detection process

4 Taking the Definitely Applicable cards, start grouping them into clusters or subcategories.

- What label would you give to each of these subcategories?

- What do these labels tell you?

Testing process

5 Looking at your profile in your selected relationship:

- What themes are emerging?

- What are you now learning?

Multiple examples

6 Now repeat the process with other relationships you have.

- What similarities are strongly emerging?

- How significant are the differences?

Model making process

- What three to five labels make up your individual profiles?

- Combining the profiles, what is the grouping of labels?

- What are you learning about who you are, as opposed to who you believe you ought to be?

26 Role Modelling

Technique devised by Fran Burgess

Based on work by Judith DeLozier

Judy DeLozier first introduced me to the use of mentors back in 1989 in Bali. As the co-creator of New Code NLP she had developed the art of deep second positioning. This is the ability to step into another's shoes as if to see the world through their eyes, hear through their ears and feel through their body. This is the essence of modelling.

THE INGREDIENTS

The Purpose
Suitable for becoming more confident in a role

The Conditions
Time: 40 mins
Resources: None
Who: G + E
Skill Level: Easy

The Delivery Method
Kinaesthetic: Spatial anchors

The NLP Frames
Neurological: Mentors, multiple perspectives
Linguistic: Neurological levels

It requires us to let go of, for that moment, what we think and feel, and just be open to the workings of the other person – mindful that we always fully return to ourselves whenever we choose.

It astonished me that I could somehow draw on the wisdom of others without actually talking to them. What was even more surprising was the fact I could call on people who may have passed on, who I didn't even know or who were historical or fictional.

As your Explorers will discover, words will come into their mouths leaving them wondering, 'Where did that come from!'

In this particular use of mentors, I have combined them with the top end of the neurological levels so that Explorers can investigate a role they are possibly uncertain about. Equally, they could use a situation, a skill or a belief as the source of their exploration. Whatever they use, I suspect they will be in for a surprise!

40 MIN G + E EASY

The Technique

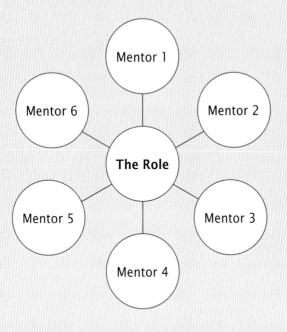

Mentor 1

Mentor 6

Mentor 2

The Role

Mentor 5

Mentor 3

Mentor 4

- What is important?

- Who are you in this role? What are you like?

- How does this role fuel your purpose?

1 Identify a role that you want to strengthen.

- How strong do you feel you are at the moment in this role? (1 low–10 high)

2 Stand in the centre and think of up to six people who have something to say about this role. These individuals could be known or unknown to you, alive or dead, real or fictional. If, for example, you want to be a stronger leader, then you might choose from Winston Churchill, Vivienne Westwood, Richard Branson, Gandalf or Harry Potter.

3 Place each of them around you. One by one, step into their space and, as them, answer the following questions:

- What do you strongly believe about this role?

4 As you gather the information from each person, return to your centre spot and acknowledge what each has offered. Once all the mentors have spoken, now ask yourself the same questions:

- What do you strongly believe now in this role?

- What is important now?

- Who are you in this role? What are you like now?

- What fuels your purpose now?

5 Imagine a situation in the near future when you will be called upon in this role.

- What are you now aware of?

- What are other people noticing?

- How strong do you now feel in this role? (1 low–10 high)

27 Developing a Part

Technique devised by Fran Burgess

Based on the work of James Lawley and Penny Tompkins

This technique is an ingenious combination of sources. It starts with identifying a part of you, or an archetype, that you want to strengthen. This may be a function, like your practical part that gets things done. Or you may have a sense that you don't have enough warrior energy to give you the stamina and resilience you need.

THE INGREDIENTS

The Purpose
Suitable for building a
particular aspect of self

The Conditions
Time: 30 mins
Resources: None
Who: G + E
Skill Level: Medium

The Delivery Method
Cognitive: Questions
Visual: Drawings

The NLP Frames
Neurological: Metaphor
Linguistic: Clean Language

Then it uses the Clean Language questions identified by James Lawley and Penny Tompkins from their modelling of David Groves. James and Penny went on to develop the hugely fertile field of Symbolic Modelling – a tremendous contribution to our understanding of internal structure.

The process starts off with your Explorer discovering the metaphor he or she associates with the chosen identity. You will discover that your Explorer will have a unique handle on how this particular identity is expressed, and that there is no 'right' answer. Taking the example of Warrior, the metaphor may be a long distance runner an indefatigable team member or someone who stands up to bullies. Whatever metaphor is selected, everything is then based around this throughout the whole process.

Encourage your Explorers to let their minds freely roam and allow whatever comes up to come up. Be prepared to be surprised. Why choose to be bored with what you already know?

Finally your Explorers are asked to draw a representation of their answers. Even more information may emerge for them at this point.

The Technique

1 Take an archetype or part which you don't feel is up to strength:

- How strong is your sense of this part at the moment? (1 low–10 high)

2 Now begin to answer the following questions, allowing whatever thought comes into your mind to stay. Resist the temptation to be rational!

Ask the Guide to record the answers – word for word.

3 When you are this identity:

- You are like what? What metaphor describes you best?

- Call this X.

4 Focusing on your metaphor:

- What is it like? Does it have a size, shape, etc.? Is there anything else about it?

- Where is X? Whereabouts?

- Is anything connected to X? How are they connected? Is there a relationship between them?

5 Continue to focus on your metaphor and the information that is emerging:

- What was before X? And what was before that?

- Where is the source of X? What is it like?

- How does this source connect with the present?

6 Finally:

- What would you rather have as X?

- What has to happen for this to happen? What else?

- Can it? (If no, go back to above question.)

7 Now draw all your images, showing the links between them. Gain a sense of how all of this connects with the archetype or part you are developing.

8 Imagine a situation that calls for this archetype.

- How is this different to similar situations in the past?

- How strong is your sense of this archetype now? (1 low–10 high)

28 Deciding Your Goal

Technique devised by Fran Burgess

This is a gentle recipe to get you started, since everything begins with an outcome, or goal.

THE INGREDIENTS

The Purpose
Suitable for getting out of a stuck state and unsupportive thoughts

The Conditions
Time: 10 mins
Resources: None
Who: E or G + E
Skill Level: Easy

The Delivery Method
Cognitive: Questions

The NLP Frames
Neurological: Multiple perspectives, time
Linguistic: Milton Model, temporal predicates

We all can get into stuck situations where we just seem to be going round and round, not getting anywhere, putting lots of energy into going forward. We might even be able to convince ourselves that we are working really hard at it. But we don't seem to get anywhere.

Unsticking ourselves doesn't have to require great effort.

What can be experienced through this technique are nudges into different time frames. These are combined with the 'loosening' effects of permissive trance language developed and perfected by Milton Erickson, the psychotherapist who devised a uniquely permissive and practical approach to accessing the unconscious mind through language. His approaches and methodology have informed much of NLP's linguistic thinking.

Explorers can either work with a partner to offer the questions – the better option since this leaves them free to just wander within their own mind. Or they can read them themselves, which is not so effective because it can be distracting and interrupt the flow of awareness.

The Technique

1 Think of the stuck situation, which may involve just you personally or a group that you are part of, at work, home or socially. Make sure that it is a goal that you really want and which will be of benefit to all.

2 Restate your goal.

- How stuck are you? (1 low–10 high)

- What objections ('Yes-Buts') come forward?

3 Come up with your own answers. Here are some examples to direct your thinking:

- I don't know if I can cope.

- In the moment, other things are more important.

- I'm not sure it is me.

4 Sit comfortably, and listen as you are read the following words:

The Guide needs to read this in a soft, slow fairytale voice – even if the words don't make sense!

- And you might not know if you can cope, and you might know, and you may not know now, and you may know now. Whatever, this is a goal that's good to pursue.

- Other things might be more important, and this might be more important, and it may be more important tomorrow, or today. Whatever, this is a goal that's good to pursue.

- And you might not know if it is you, and you may know it is you, and others may not know and they may know that it is you. Whatever, this is a goal that's good to pursue.

5 Take a moment now to notice:

- What has shifted?

- What new thoughts you are having?

- What might now be possible?

6 If there are any further objections, then go through Step 3 once more.

7 As a result of this process:

- How stuck are you? (1 low–10 high)

8 And finally:

- You may act upon this now, or you may leave it for a time, or you may do something else. Whatever, this is a goal that's good.

29 Finding Purpose

Technique devised by Fran Burgess

As children we gained much of our learning through stories – from tales specifically written for children, from family folklore and handed-down anecdotes, from talk overheard whilst unobserved.

THE INGREDIENTS

The Purpose
Suitable for exploring a sense of purpose

The Conditions
Time: 10 mins
Resources: None
Who: E
Skill Level: Easy

The Delivery Method
Auditory: Stories and anecdotes

The NLP Frames
Neurological: None
Linguistic: Milton Model

Some of the greatest teachers taught through stories – the parables of Jesus, the fables of Aesop and the epic tales of mythology and saga. Some indigenous cultures have a completely aural tradition, passing on their lineage and legacy through chanting, music and song.

Milton Erickson based much of his later therapeutic work on the process of storytelling, where the structure of the story and the nature of the content would mirror the class of problem and the class of solution.

This technique devotes itself to the process of offering selected tales to activate inner learning and widen a receptive awareness. I have put together a short selection of stories, compiled from events that have happened to me, anecdotes offered by my teachers, observations from radio or TV and poetry. The theme connecting them all is awareness of one's individual purpose. I could just as easily have concentrated on a state, a belief or a problem.

This approach has infinite applications, as all good storytellers know. You can offer this technique conversationally, stringing the different stories together. You could read it off the page. You could illustrate some of it with images or a PowerPoint slide, which would be calling in the visual representation system as well.

The Technique

1. How is it that the first question a child learns to ask is 'Why?' Followed by 'When?' and 'Where'? Rarely 'How?' So how is it that children know so early on the importance of purpose?

2. Bill O'Hanlon, the prolific author from the field of therapy, and also incidentally Milton Erickson's one-time gardener, has a theory that our purpose stems from one of four sources or from a combination of them. He maintains that the energy that fuels our purpose will have its source in these childhood experiences:

   - Pissed: when something or someone made us so angry that we vowed we would do something about it when we were grown up.

   - Blissed: for the few of us who came into this world already knowing our purpose and have a running start on our mission.

   - Dissed: when we were discounted, ignored and rejected and we sought to recognise and sponsor others.

   - Blessed: when our being was recognised and rewarded by a grown-up and we resolved to touch others in the same way.

3. To live without a sense of purpose, known or hinted at, renders our life meaningless and our goals, outcomes and decisions futile. We are just going through the motions. This is never more powerfully expressed than in the words of Mary Oliver, in her majestic poem 'When Death Comes': 'I don't want to end up simply having visited this world.'

4. David Gordon, in his Meaningful Existence Model, approaches the sense of purpose from a different angle. He maintains that we naturally exemplify our purpose, even if we don't recognise it as such. He invites you to look at instances where you were at your most natural best, both as a child and as an adult. As you recall these events, when you couldn't not be who you are, you will recognise that themes and constants emerge. You will notice that the values that come to light are those that drive you. These form your purpose. Looking back at your life, you will notice that it has been motivated to fulfil this, and those special moments have been when you achieved it.

5. Robert Dilts suggests that our Purpose is made up of the combination of our vision, what we want to achieve that is beyond us: our mission, which is our unique contribution to this; our ambition, which is the performance or status we want to achieve; and our role, which is who we want to be in this endeavour. Where does this take your thinking?

6. The Hawaiians believe that we come into this world knowing our purpose, but we forget it just after birth. They also believe that we choose our parents since they will provide us with the vehicle to achieve this purpose. Off we go on our life's journey, loosely talking about being on our path or straying from our path, not necessarily knowing what the path is or where it leads. The further we stray the more out of sorts and depressed we become. In the film *Little Big Man* the mantra of the old Indian Chief was 'It's a good day to die.' How often have we had moments

when, if the Great Hand came down and plucked us up into the sky, we would offer no resistance? These are moments of being in our purpose.

7 Harry Chapin, the musician and visionary who died tragically young, had inscribed on his gravestone the chorus of his song 'I Wonder What Would Happen to This World':

Now if a man tried
To take his time on Earth
And prove before he died
What one man's life could be worth
I wonder what would happen
to this world.

Task

1 Using Bill O'Hanlon's model, take a moment to establish the possible sources of your mission.

2 Consider instances in your life where you were proud and pleased with your behaviour. What characteristics were you demonstrating? What was important for you? How is this still important for you today?

3 Think of times when you felt at peace. Conversely, think of those moments when you were most out of sorts. What needs were being met or not met? What does this now tell you about your purpose?

4 What lies outside of you that concerns you? And what unique contribution do you want to make towards this?

5 What inscription would you like on your gravestone?

30 Aligning Goals

Technique devised by Fran Burgess

This is a simple yet effective process which again combines a couple of techniques, illustrating how picking and mixing ingredients can produce pleasing results.

THE INGREDIENTS

The Purpose
Suitable for establishing collaborative agreement and goal setting

The Conditions
Time: 45 mins
Resources: None
Who: G + E
Skill Level: Easy

The Delivery Method
Cognitive: Questions

The NLP Frames
Neurological: Multiple perspectives
Linguistic: Outcome frame

Collaboration comes when the parties are in agreement about what is important, and therefore focus on what unites as opposed to what divides them. I was first introduced to a co-alignment process during my trainer training in Santa Cruz – we were seeking to generate constructive relationships for co-training using neurological level alignment. Rather like a zipper action, both parties work up their respective track from Environment, Behaviours, Skills, Beliefs and Values, Identity to Mission, and then through selecting similarities only, zip the two tracks together to arrive in harmony back at Environment. There is an example of this form of co-alignment in Recipe 36.

Instead of the neurological levels, here we are working through key elements of the outcome frame. And instead of having the other party working with you, you are asked to use the magic of second position to do the work instead. It is always amazing to realise just how much you know about another.

45 MIN   G + E   EASY

76

The Technique

1   Identify someone you will be working alongside on an upcoming project.

2   What is your level of confidence that this partnership will be a success? (1 low–10 high)

3   Draw up a grid with the following headings and write down the answers to these questions for yourself. Step into your partner's shoes and come up with what his or her answer might be. Allow whatever thoughts to emerge as if you are him or her. (If you really don't know, then you may like to ask him or her when you next see them.)

Question	Me	My partner

■ What do you want to gain from participating in this project? For yourself and for those affected by it?

■ How will this benefit you? Why is this important?

■ When do you/don't you want this?

> Have the Guide record the answers to the questions.

■ What has stopped you previously? What can you do differently?

■ What resources do you need? What do you already have?

■ How will you know you've been successful? What will you and others see, hear and feel?

■ If you achieved this goal would you really want it? What might you lose? Is there anything you want to make sure you can keep?

4   If you don't have total certainty on the last question, go back to the others and make whatever adjustments you need.

5   Now that you have an understanding of what is important to you and to your partner:

■ Notice the differences between you. How significant are they?

■ Notice the similarities between you. How significant are they?

■ What are you prepared to accept so that you can get what you want?

■ What are you going to ask for that is important for you?

■ What is your level of confidence that this partnership will be a success? (1 low–10 high)

31 Push and Pull

Technique devised by Steve Gilligan

I really enjoyed being introduced to this technique by Steve Gilligan during his Generative Trance workshop at the Northern School of NLP. It appeals to me on various levels.

THE INGREDIENTS

The Purpose
Suitable for detecting and removing limitation

The Conditions
Time: 10 mins
Resources: None
Who: G + E
Skill Level: Easy

The Delivery Method
Kinaesthetic: Hands, somatic syntax

The NLP Frames
Neurological: None
Linguistic: None

The workshop itself was quite amazing, provoking some impressive shifts on my part. I was contemplating making some changes in my life and some real inspiration emerged out of the processes Steve led us through. It packs a punch – if you're ready for it!

The technique itself is a lovely combination of processes. Again simple, it takes the somatic expression of an emotion and draws, literally, upon the somatic wisdom of the hands to find resolution. You will be surprised at what will emerge for you.

It is always a joy to experience the inspired alchemy of technique blended with intuition.

I'm grateful for Steve's permission to use his techniques and also for all the support and sponsorship he has shown to me over the years.

The Technique

1 Think of something you know you want to be, yet are holding back from becoming. You know you have it within you, yet there is something stopping you.

   ■ How successful do you feel you can be? (1 low–10 high)

2 Be aware of what it is you want. Devise a movement with your hands that somehow encapsulates this sense of what you want to be. Just allow your hands and arms to move as they will. Avoid being too literal. The movement might even involve your whole body. Work on this movement until it completely fits with what you desire about this possible future.

> Remind your Explorer to trust their body to come up with the answers. This is not a 'thinking' exercise.

3 Now consider what might be holding you back. As you become aware of this, once more let your hands and arms move in a way that describes this limiting feature. It's worth remembering that a limitation is usually present as a way of keeping you safe.

4 Once you have both movements appropriately practised, perform the first one and then the second one, and then return to the first one again. And so on.

5 Soon a new movement will emerge that is a combination of both of them. Let this new movement evolve and take a firm hold, so that you can fully sense the wisdom that is being expressed through your hands and your body.

6 Once you are satisfied, ask yourself:

   ■ How successful do you feel you can be? (1 low–10 high)

32 Leonardo's Arm

Technique devised by Fran Burgess

Based on work by Robert Dilts

One of many modelling projects Robert Dilts has undertaken is his fascinating work on the modelling of geniuses. Working from documentation, Robert uncovered the approaches to creative generative thinking adopted by Mozart, Walt Disney, Nikola Tesla, Albert Einstein, Sigmund Freud, Sherlock Holmes and Leonardo da Vinci.

THE INGREDIENTS

The Purpose
Suitable for exploring a particular relationship

The Conditions
Time: 20 mins
Resources: None
Who: G + E
Skill Level: Easy

The Delivery Method
Auditory: A story

The NLP Frames
Neurological: Time
Linguistic: Milton Model

You can find out all about this work in his books *Strategies of Genius 1-3*. As part of his discoveries, he identifies 20 different traits shared by these marvellous thinkers, which make for thoughtful reading. The full description of these patterns of genius can be found in the NLP Encyclopaedia at www.nlpu.com.

I've taken his work with Leonardo da Vinci and given it an auditory treatment, in the form of a trance-like story – an approach often used by Milton Erickson in his work with clients.

This is your chance to offer some gentle trance language to waft your Explorers off to some inner place. I hope you and they enjoy it.

20 MIN   G + E   EASY

The Technique

1   Identify a particular relationship you have that you want to understand more fully. It may be with another person, an object or an organisation.

2   Now sit comfortably, with both feet on the floor and your hands lightly on your lap. Allow your shoulders to drop, your jaw to relax and your eyes to close. All you need to do is listen. If you want me to give you longer to think, just raise your hand.

3   As you now become aware of this relationship you are concerned with, and the level of satisfaction you feel, you may like to explore even further its nature and composition. Or you may be interested in receiving new information which would give you what you are looking for. Or you may welcome insight into the contributions which created this particular outcome that you have.

Speak slowly and gently.

4   Because relationships are very curious things. They may not be what they seem ... have differing interpretations ... be operating within the realms of harsh reality or soft fantasy, or somewhere else entirely. Where might yours be now that you notice?

5   Leonardo da Vinci, when he was working on understanding the intricacies of an arm, would spend many many hours laboriously studying the anatomy of many arms, to find out how an arm develops from its infancy to the inevitable withering of old age. He would be fascinated to know the moments of transition from one form to another and which element would begin to age first. He eventually was able to predict how most arms grow and change, and so notice what was unique to a particular arm.

6   And so with relationships. What similarities do your relationships share? How do they differ? What do you notice about how they start and grow? What stops them from growing? What is their rate of development? How do they end? What might cause them to end?

7   Leonardo would often liken the arm to another object, like a plant, and seek to find comparisons between both systems. Today you might choose a car, and so the muscle becomes the engine, the bone the chassis, the blood the fuel. This way, he was able to understand the interrelationships between each of the elements. He understood that there are many links and connections within any object. He understood the constant series of cause and effect, the two-way flow of information, the value placed on each transaction, and how each of these actions increased, decreased, or remained the same over time. He understood the hidden dynamics, operating below the surface, which contributed to the effectiveness of functioning.

8   And so you could also liken your particular relationship to a specific object, and begin to find out for yourself the ingredients – how these are connected, the importance of each in themselves and with the other elements. You may also notice which elements are more used than others, which are beginning to become worn,

which are underused, and which pieces are missing. This is such a fascinating system.

9   Each of us is unique in our own special way, with our own special contribution to offer, whilst in turn we receive the contributions from others. And as with all gifts, some we welcome and some we politely put to one side. We know it's possible to choose our response and what to do next, don't we?

10 So as you are considering what might be the invisible connections within your relationship, which keeps it together or eases it apart, and you understand more clearly how this relationship is evolving and growing into whatever it now needs to be, you will also have an awareness of what you now need to do, to tend it in a way that keeps it healthy and wise, keeps you healthy and wise.

11 You can do this now, couldn't you? That was possible, wasn't it? And isn't it good to provide something that is right for both you and the other person, yourself?

33 Surviving a Relationship

Technique devised by Fran Burgess

Based on work by Ernest Rossi

This process emerged from a therapy session. The client was working through the pain of a relationship coming to an end. This begged a timeline process, but I remember that I was feeling tired and I knew I didn't have the energy to be on my feet for three quarters of an hour. Happily I had noticed that when he was talking about himself his right hand was dominant, which triggered the light bulb moment and so a new process was born!

THE INGREDIENTS

The Purpose
Suitable for plotting the journey through the end of a relationship

The Conditions
Time: 30 mins
Resources: None
Who: G + F
Skill Level: Advanced

The Delivery Method
Kinaesthetic: Hands, somatic syntax

The NLP Frames
Neurological: Time, multiple perspectives
Linguistic: Spatial predicates, temporal predicates

I had been to an Ernest Rossi workshop a couple of months earlier, and had played around with his fascinating work with hands quite a few times since then. If you search online for Homunculus, you will find a strange image of a misshapen man. This represents the relationship between various parts of our body and the number of neural connections they generate in our cortex – the part of our brain associated with thought and action. Our hands win hands down! Rossi would have it that working directly with the neurology of our hands leads to constructing new neural pathways, and so effecting change.

The process here is a combination of timeline, somatic syntax and the duality of hands – letting the hands describe through action the desired journey towards resolution.

Make sure your explorers allow their hands to move freely. No putting them where they think they ought to be! Just let the hands travel in their own sweet way and trust the wisdom inherent in their neurology.

30 MIN   G + F   ADVANCED

The Technique

1 Taking the relationship that has ended, let your dominant hand represent you, and your other hand your partner.

   ■ How optimistic are you about your future? (1 low–10 high)

2 Sitting down, clear a space on a table in front of you. Take both your hands and bring them near to your body. Place them to represent the two of you when you first met. Now slowly, let them travel forwards independently to arrive at today. One hand may rise above or fall below the other. One may move quicker, or closer or further away than the other.

   ■ What is the space like between your hands? This represents the closeness or distance between you.

   ■ What speed does each hand move at? Differences represent the different rates of personal growth between you.

3 Take a moment to make sense of this information. You can go back and rehearse it further, making any minor or micro adjustments until it becomes a realistic representation of your relationship.

4 Now move your dominant hand forward in a way that describes how you want yourself to be in the future. Practise this till it feels just right, adjusting the speed and location – up, down, side to side.

5 Now move your other hand forward in a way that describes how you want your ex-partner to be in the future. Practise this till it feels just right, once more adjusting the speed and location. Make sure your movement reflects honourable intention.

6 Once you are certain of the movement of both hands, move them both at the same time. Repeat this at least five or six times so that you gain a real sense of how things are going to be for you.

7 Now ask yourself:

   ■ How optimistic are you now about your future? (1 low–10 high)

34 Where Am I Here?

Technique devised by Fran Burgess

This simple trance process seeks to help you explore your relationship with your relationship, if that doesn't sound too weird.

THE INGREDIENTS

The Purpose
Suitable for creating choice and options within a relationship

The Conditions
Time: 20 mins
Resources: None
Who: G + E
Skill Level: Easy

The Delivery Method
Auditory: Guided visualisation

The NLP Frames
Neurological: Metaphor, space, time
Linguistic: Milton Model, spatial predicates, temporal predicates

Whenever there is you and another person or thing, you will have a relationship. It may be good, bad, serving, detracting, supportive, unsupportive, steady, unstable, escalating or decreasing. There is also the chicken and egg scenario: whatever we feel *about* the relationship will directly affect the dynamics *within* it, and the dynamics will inform our emotional responses.

The other factor to consider is that we can only directly influence our own contribution to a relationship, since the actions of others are outside our control – despite what we might sometimes think!

Through exploring the dynamics of space and working with metaphor, your Explorers are invited to travel in-between the links that connect them to their own particular relationship, so that they gain a clearer sense of what is happening. This leaves them with greater choices about what to do next.

20 MIN   G + E   EASY

86

The Technique

1 Take a moment now to relax and become as comfortable as you choose to be. For some this may mean sitting up and closing your eyes, making sure your legs and hands are uncrossed. Or you may prefer to lie down, or keep your eyes open. Whatever you choose to do is fine.

2 You are aware of a relationship that you are involved in which does not give you satisfaction. You may sense a lack of some important value.

3 Take a moment to find a metaphor which sums up your relationship. Is it a sinking ship, a runaway train, a seesaw?

4 Once you have identified a metaphor which feels right for you, now consider:

   ■ What happens when you step into this metaphor? What do you notice? Where is the energy? Where does it flow or stop? What catches your attention in particular? What makes you curious? What is out of sight? What might be confusing?

Read this in a slow gentle way, giving Explorers plenty of time to explore between the paragraphs.

   ■ Which part represents your contribution? And which part represents the other's contribution? What do you notice about this? What happens when these contributions alter? Explore different ways of doing this and, as you do so, notice which choices feel better or make things worse.

   ■ How does this metaphor form and grow? What sustains it? How might it become something else?

   ■ What is it like being on the outside looking into or onto this metaphor? What do you notice? What surrounds it, lies below it, exists above it? What different ways are there to get into the metaphor, or out of it?. Take a moment now to explore just how you might do that.

   ■ Now consider your relative contributions, within the metaphor. How are these contributions connected? How is each in service to the other – or not? What metaphor now sums up the way these contributions can become harmonious? For example, oil to get the cogs moving easily. Notice which contribution takes the lead, and when the lead changes. What sort of dance is created? What music would support this dance? Follow the dance and notice what happens.

   ■ How might all of this influence the nature of your relationship? Take a moment to listen to the voice of new learning that becomes available.

   ■ What are your intentions now regarding your relationship? What do you want your purpose to be now?

35 It Takes Two

Technique devised by Fran Burgess

A card sort combines kinaesthetic and visual thinking, and the process of trial and error can be very satisfying once the cards have found their rightful places. In the process you find your hands moving cards intuitively, before your head has kicked into place.

THE INGREDIENTS

The Purpose
Suitable for exploring what direction to take in an emotional relationship

The Conditions
Time: 15 mins
Resources: Printed and blank cards
Who: G + E
Skill Level: Easy

The Delivery Method
Cognitive: Card sort

The NLP Frames
Neurological: Metaphor
Linguistic: None

In this technique, the card sort is being used to explore the sort of relationship we want. It can be a romantic relationship, one of parenting, work, social or friendship. If we detect something lacking in the relationship we have, we will be consciously or unconsciously comparing it against a desired ideal. Working with the cards makes it very easy to explore something that might otherwise be difficult and provoke strong emotions, because the cards let us become more detached and distanced.

Often your Explorers may not start off without a clear idea of what they would rather have. Encourage them to come up with as many different types of pairings – the more bizarre the merrier – since this card sort helps tease out the elements that are being looked for and confirms what is already desirable.

The Technique

1 Consider the personal relationship in question.

2 How certain are you of the direction you want to take? (1 low–10 high)

3 Write as many examples of pairs as you can think of on separate cards. Here are some examples to get you thinking (you will find a pre-printed version in Appendix 1 which you can photocopy and cut up).

Sugar and spice	Horse and hounds	Hearts and minds
Horse and cart	Dog and bone	King and country
Ship and sail	Fish and chips	Tom and Jerry
Sea and shore	Tooth and claw	Torvill and Dean
Ducks and drakes	Wood and trees	Bonnie and Clyde
Heads and tails	Fine and dandy	North and south

4 Add any more examples of your own using the blanks provided.

5 Sort the cards instinctively into three piles:

■ Pairings that feel good.

■ Pairings that leave you neutral.

■ Pairings you don't like.

6 Look at all the pairings in the pile that you like:

■ What do they have in common?

■ What themes are emerging?

■ What words describe these pairings?

■ What in particular appeals to you?

7 Taking this information:

■ How does this compare now with the relationship that you have?

8 Given this understanding:

■ What options do you now have?

■ What can you do differently?

■ What do you no longer need?

9 How certain are you of the direction you want to take? (1 low–10 high)

36 Co-aligning Conflict

Technique devised by Fran Burgess

Based on work by Robert Dilts

I was in Paris in the early 1980s when there was a large demonstration in Les Invalides – of disaffected teachers as it turned out. I was initially drawn to the incredible number of riot police vans congregating around the huge square and I was really eager to get a closer look to see what was happening.

THE INGREDIENTS

The Purpose
Suitable for overcoming internal conflict

The Conditions
Time: 30 mins
Resources: None
Who: G + E
Skill Level: Medium

The Delivery Method
Kinaesthetic: Spatial anchors

The NLP Frames
Neurological: Neurological levels, parts
Linguistic: None

However, at the same time, I was more than somewhat intimidated by the fierceness of the riot police with all their helmets, shields and batons – an unfamiliar sight in the UK at that time. Both responses seemed to be present in equal measure, which made for tentative exploring.

If I could bring these two Parts together and draw on the strength of both, I would be a far more consistent explorer and learner. Your Explorers may have similarly conflicting Parts that prevent them from being the carer, leader or sportsman they want to be.

Taking the co-alignment process mentioned in the Aligning Goals technique (Recipe 30), this time I'm using Robert Dilts's inspired neurological levels. With this approach, you'll find your Explorers can gain new understanding of the nature of the conflicting Parts operating within them and in so doing come together on the similarities these Parts share.

Some of you may be asking, 'Why not do a Visual Squash or a Pull and Push technique?' Well, this approach generates far more cognitive information, as opposed to 'just' the somatic information, which works at an unconscious level.

I've suggested working on a tabletop as an alternative to a big scale floor approach. There are two elements here so using both hands also introduces the physiology favoured by Ernest Rossi. How good is that?

The Technique

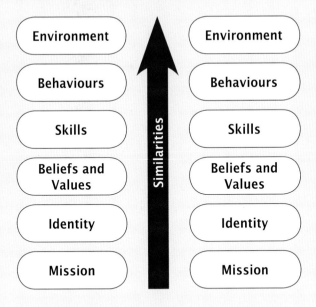

1. Think of a situation where you are pulled in opposing directions, and this reduces your effectiveness in a role.

   ■ How would you rate your performance in this role? (1 low–10 high)

2. Set out a space on the table in front of you so that your fingers can 'walk' backwards and forwards up and down the levels. Make sure your Environment space is furthest away from you.

3. Identify the two significant parts within you that are in conflict. Identify the environment in which you want to be effective. Choose which part you want to start with.

4. Answer the following sequence of questions, using your left hand for the first part and work your way up the levels. It is useful to have someone to record your answers.

   ■ Environment: What are you currently seeing, hearing and feeling in this environment?

   ■ Behaviours: What are you doing in this environment?

   ■ Skills: What skills are you using to enable you to do these things?

   ■ Beliefs and Values: What beliefs are supporting these skills? What is important for you?

   ■ Identity: When you are this Part what are you like? What metaphor sums you up?

   ■ Mission: What else is important to you? What purpose is being served by your identity?

5. Now do the same with your right hand for the second part.

6. Having gathered the information for both parts, now bring both hands to the point between the Mission for both. Walk both hands down this connecting space, identifying the similarities shared at each level.

7. When you arrive back at Environment:

   ■ What do you notice now? What are you seeing, hearing and feeling?

   ■ How would you rate your performance in this role? (1 low–10 high)

37 Sponsoring Another

Technique devised by Fran Burgess

Model devised by Steve Gilligan

Steve Gilligan has been promoting the concept of sponsorship for his many years as a psychotherapist. He was weaned on the concept of utilisation and permission, which were the hallmarks of Erickson's approach. His thinking is also deeply influenced by his lifelong involvement in aikido – a martial art in which you go with the energy flow generated by the attacker instead of resisting or attempting to combat it. What you resist persists.

THE INGREDIENTS

The Purpose
Suitable for strengthening personal effectiveness

The Conditions
Time: 15 mins
Resources: None
Who: E
Skill Level: Easy

The Delivery Method
Kinaesthetic: Spatial anchors

The NLP Frames
Neurological: Anchoring
Linguistic: None

Wherever there is something that we want to suppress or hide or that we recoil from when we see it in another, our tendency is to instinctively want to remove it, banish it and protect ourselves from it. For Steve, it is quite the reverse. For him, the secret is to stay open, come alongside it and work with its energy. Through befriending it and understanding how it fits into the overall system, we can arrive in a new generative position – where difference and change is possible.

He suggests that there are three attitudes involved in sponsorship which complement each other.

- Tender: This is similar to the way you talk to a baby or a dog – when no one is listening! Useful when someone is being too hard on themselves.

- Fierce: This is a sense of being steadfast and strong – a protector not an aggressor. Useful for standing your ground and being firm with the other when they are being too tender with themselves and unable to hold fast.

- Playful: This is a childlike sense of joyous frivolity and lightness, since nothing is too serious to take too seriously.

Some of these states we have in abundance – sometimes too much which can get in the way of our effectiveness. Conversely we may find that we are depleted in one of them. We need to develop our access to these states and increase our flexibility, so that we can enhance our ability to sponsor effectively.

The Technique

1 Think of a situation you want to be more equipped to deal with.

- How confident are you about dealing with it? (1 low–10 high)

2 Establish three spaces on the floor to represent:

- Tender: similar to the way you talk to a baby, or a dog – when no one is listening in! Useful when someone is being too hard on themselves

- Fierce: a sense of being steadfast and strong, a protector not an aggressor. Useful for standing your ground and being firm with the other, when they are being too tender with themselves and unable to hold fast.

- Playful: a sense of joyous frivolity and lightness, since nothing is too serious to take too seriously.

3 Step into each space and remember a time when you experienced something similar to each of these descriptions.

- What are you seeing, hearing and feeling?

- Where is the sensation in your body?

- What is it like? (e.g. a lava lamp, body armour, an imp)

4 Stay with each one until the sensation is really strong then step out of the space and give yourself a shake, so that you no longer have a sense of that sensation. Then step into the next space.

5 Once you have a clear bodily description of all three states, go back to Tender and re-access your tenderness. Move directly on to Fierce, bringing the first state with you, and access your fierceness. Now bring both states with you into Playful and access your playfulness as well.

6 Take this combination and capture it in a gesture with images and sound.

7 Now return to the situation you want to be more equipped to deal with.

- How confident are you now? (1 low–10 high)

- What might you consider doing differently?

38 Fine Tuning Sponsorship

Technique devised by Fran Burgess

Model devised by Steve Gilligan

Models don't have to be restricted to only one treatment. Imagine if there was only one way to cook chicken – there would be far fewer cookbooks on the shelves and some very boring dinners. It would also mean there was no way to accommodate differing tastes and cuisines. Such a lack of imagination would be responsible for denying the possibilities for cooking the chicken in a variety of ways using different ingredients and accompanying foods.

THE INGREDIENTS

The Purpose
Suitable for improving own contribution to relationships

The Conditions
Time: 20 mins
Resources: None
Who: G + E
Skill Level: Easy

The Delivery Method
Kinaesthetic: Sliding scales

The NLP Frames
Neurological: Submodalities
Linguistic: None

This recipe (and Recipe 39), demonstrates that a model can give birth to many different experiences, depending on what you want to achieve. By changing the cooking method, and introducing different ingredients, one model can be a source for multiple experiences as the end result.

In this instance, by introducing the notion of sliding scales, like faders on a mixing desk, we can naturally change the structure and composition of the states involved. It is fascinating what differences you can experience not just through increasing and decreasing the intensity of a state, but also by shifting them in relation to each other.

It is remarkable how the balance directly contributes to the outcome. In this example, if playfulness is absent, then fierceness can become destructive. If there is insufficient fierceness then tenderness can become self-indulgent. While too much playfulness can lead to misplaced frivolity.

Getting the balance right can really jump-start a relationship into becoming constructive and productive.

The Technique

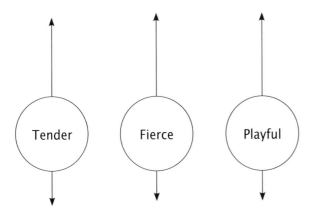

1 Take a moment to access your own internal description of each state.

- Tender: A sense of softness similar to the way you talk to a baby or a dog – when no one is listening!

- Fierce: A sense of being steadfast and strong – a protector not an aggressor.

- Playful: A sense of joyous fun and lightness.

- Notice which ones are easy to access and which are more difficult. If needs be, go to some of the earlier techniques in the book to help you make each state as strong as the others.

2 Think of a relationship that is currently unsatisfactory or that has been unsatisfactory for some time.

- How satisfactory is this relationship? (1 low–10 high)

3 Register on your mixing desk your starting point for each state.

- Tenderness   1 2 3 4 5 6 7 8 9 10
- Fierceness   1 2 3 4 5 6 7 8 9 10
- Playfulness   1 2 3 4 5 6 7 8 9 10

4 Begin to move the sliding knob for each state up and down the scale until it seems to fit with what is more appropriate and likely to pay dividends for you. You can decrease as well as increase the intensity of each state. Too much can be just as harmful as too little. Stifling caring can inhibit as much as constant flippancy.

5 Once you have the mix right, take yourself into a situation you know is coming up with this person.

- How are you responding? What are you doing differently?

- What differences are you noticing in the other person?

- How satisfactory does the relationship seem now? (1 low–10 high)

39 Developing Your Inner Coach

Technique devised by Fran Burgess

Model devised by Steve Gilligan

Alongside Recipes 37 and 38 here is another way to work with Steven Gilligan's fabulous model. This Recipe goes to show how easy it is to pick and mix components and processes to create distinctive effects.

THE INGREDIENTS

The Purpose
Suitable for developing an inner coach

The Conditions
Time: 20 mins
Resources: None
Who: G + E
Skill Level: Easy

The Delivery Method
Kinaesthetic: Spatial anchors
Cognitive: Relational constructs

The NLP Frames
Neurological: Parts
Linguistic: None

By turning the model into a triangle, we create an enclosed system that allows for the development of an emergent property held within it. From within this relational field new insight can emerge. The energy created comes not just from the mix of each of the elements, but also by the relationship and the transition points between one and the other – a pretty fertile space.

You will also notice what happens when you mix the words around, which is similar to the Confusion Technique in Building Excellence (Recipe 10). This helps to expand the relational field and widen the source of new information. To paraphrase Einstein: 'You have to go to the edge of the problem space to discover the solution space. You can't use the same thinking that constructed the problem to find the solution.'

Whilst you can do this technique sitting down and working with it intellectually, I would recommend that you get up and mark out the space on the floor. You will get a far better result – and possibly a few surprises.

20 MIN

G + E

EASY

The Technique

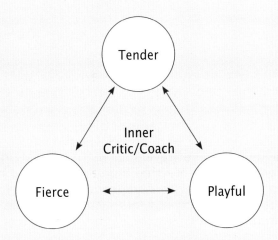

Tender

Inner Critic/Coach

Fierce   Playful

3 Step into one space and face the other two. Taking the different permutations, what are the appropriate levels of each that you need to support the development of this part?

Tenderly tender	Fiercely fierce	Playfully playful
Tenderly fierce	Fiercely tender	Playfully fierce
Tenderly playful	Fiercely playful	Playfully tender

1 Take a moment to access your own internal description of each state. Notice which ones are easy to access and which are more difficult.

■ Tender: Similar to the way you talk to a baby or a dog – when no one is listening!

■ Fierce: A sense of being steadfast and strong – a protector not an aggressor.

■ Playful: A sense of joyous frivolity and lightness.

2 Step into the centre and access your Inner Critic – the part of you that puts you down and really gives you a hard time when it thinks you have done something wrong.

■ What sorts of things does it say?

■ What is its complaint?

■ What part of you does it think is responsible for the behaviour?

■ How resourceful do you feel?
(1 low–10 high)

4 Once you have explored the full space and know where the balance lies between each of the states, step once more into the middle.

■ What is the response now of your Inner Critic?

■ What would happen if you renamed it as your Inner Coach?

■ What can it now be saying to the part responsible for the behaviour?

■ How resourceful do you now feel?
(1 low–10 high)

5 Now select three situations where you would expect your Inner Critic to step in and demoralise you. Applying your understanding of sponsorship:

■ What is happening now in this situation?

■ How effective are you now becoming?

40 Conflict Resolution

Technique devised by Fran Burgess

Model devised by Kenneth Thomas and Ralph Kilmann

This model, known as the Thomas-Kilmann Conflict Mode Instrument, developed by Kenneth Thomas and Ralph Kilmann, indentifies five modes for handling conflict. A student introduced it to me, and, as ever when I meet a new model, my ears prick up and my nose twitches. To my delight it led me to some interesting email exchanges with Ken Thomas, who kindly gave me permission for its use.

THE INGREDIENTS

The Purpose
Suitable for creating new possibilities in a relationship

The Conditions
Time: 30 mins
Resources: None
Who: G + E
Skill Level: Easy

The Delivery Method
Cognitive: Questions

The NLP Frames
Neurological: None
Linguistic: What, How, Why

The model illustrates how low cooperation and low assertiveness results in avoidance; high cooperation and low assertiveness results in accommodation; high assertiveness and low cooperation results in competition; and high cooperation and high assertiveness results in collaboration. The midpoint between them all is the zone of compromise.

I have developed a couple of recipes around this model to show what is possible as well as providing you with useful experiences to work with.

In this first recipe, I presupposed that the effects of avoidance would be withdrawal, accommodation would be loss of identity, and competition would be alienation. I then used these felt senses to discover if the undesirable effects of conflict management have gone over threshold. Offering a What, How, Why sequence to address the levels of cooperation and assertiveness then opens up the exploration of the compromise space.

30 MIN   G + E   EASY

The Technique

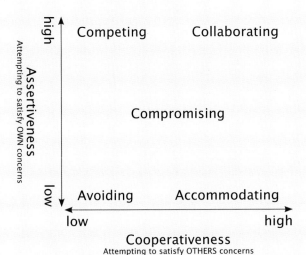

Assertiveness
Attempting to satisfy OWN concerns

high — Competing   Collaborating

Compromising

low — Avoiding   Accommodating

low   high

Cooperativeness
Attempting to satisfy OTHERS concerns

Adapted from Kenneth W. Thomas (1976), 'Conflict and conflict management', in Marvin D. Dunnette (ed.) *Handbook of Industrial and Organizational Psychology* (Chicago: Rand McNally), p. 900.

1   Identify a situation where you are required to achieve a set outcome with someone with whom you have a real difficulty working.

- How satisfactory is this relationship? (1 low–10 high)

2   Looking at this situation, I find that:

- I am withdrawing   YES/NO
- I am feeling alienated YES/NO
- I am denying my self   YES/NO

3   My evidence of this is …

4   Where you have said yes, consider the following questions:

- How much are you compromising yourself?
- How are you not considering the concerns of the other?
- How are you not giving voice to your own concerns?

- How is it that your concerns are more important than the other person's?
- How are you putting his or her concerns before your own?
- How are unable to acknowledge what either of you really want?

5   Now remind yourself of your *joint goal*. You may need a moment to work out what your joint goal actually is.

- What has brought you both together – to achieve what?
- Is this goal still relevant? Is it still shared? If not, what is more realistic?
- What is important about this goal?
- How would acknowledging your concerns and the concerns of the other make a difference to the goal?
- Why would this be important?

6   Given what you now understand about this relationship, and your response both to asking for yourself and to letting others state their needs:

- What do you need to do?
- How will he or she know you are seeking a collaborative outcome, involving both of you?
- How satisfactory can this relationship become? (1 low–10 high)

41 Healthy Compromise

Technique devised by Fran Burgess

Model devised by Kenneth Thomas and Ralph Kilmann

Here is another recipe based on the Thomas-Kilmann model used in the previous technique (Recipe 40).

THE INGREDIENTS

The Purpose
Suitable for working towards conflict resolution

The Conditions
Time: 30 mins
Resources: None
Who: G + E
Skill Level: Easy

The Delivery Method
Kinaesthetic: Spatial anchors
Cognitive: Relational constructs

The NLP Frames
Neurological: None
Linguistic: None

Instead of using the term *compromise* as a form of conflict resolution, where there is equal give and take within an issue, I have opted to use it as a way of feeling. Within conflict situations, we can often find ourselves being compromised or compromising ourselves. Either way, we know we have given away too much of ourselves – even if we don't know exactly what that is.

It is really important that we notice the first signs of this discomfort – to alert us to the necessity of reconnecting with our own needs or the needs of others. Discovering what it feels like somatically when we have overly compromised our own spirit, and discounted the spirit in another, gives us early warning signals to do something different – if, that is, we want to *really* achieve our mutual goal.

I have focused on the interface between compromise and the over-use of the other four conflict styles (accommodation, collaboration, avoidance and competition), the thinking being that when we no longer feel compromised, we have a choice on how we can manage the conflict.

I have set up a closed system through triangulating the model, thereby creating a positive relational field within which healthy compromise can grow. Using the characteristics of each style and weaving them in with their partner's creates a form of confusion which loosens up the system and opens it to new possibilities. It certainly blurs the edges of inevitability.

The Technique

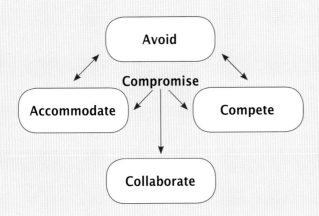

1 Identify a situation where you are required to achieve a set outcome with someone with whom you have a real difficulty working.

2 Stand in the centre, the Compromise space, face each of the spaces and ask yourself:

■ What level of compromise are you feeling? (1 low–10 high)

■ How much space do you feel you have in this space?

3 Step into the Avoid space. In this situation:

■ How are you avoiding accommodating? What could you more usefully do?

■ How are you avoiding competing? What could you more usefully do?

■ How are you avoiding collaborating? What could you more usefully do?

4 Step into the Accommodate space. In this situation:

■ How are you accommodating avoidance? What could you more usefully do?

■ How are you accommodating competition? What could you more usefully do?

■ How are you accommodating non-collaboration? What could you more usefully do?

5 Step into the Compete space. In this situation:

■ How can you compete assertively?

■ How can you compete cooperatively?

■ How can you compete collaboratively?

6 Now return to the Compromise space.

■ What are you gaining that you didn't have before?

■ What have you let go of that no longer matters? Why is this important?

7 Given what you now understand about this relationship, set up your contract:

■ You will only compromise yourself through avoidance if …

■ You will only compromise yourself through accommodation when …

■ You will only compromise yourself through competition should …

8 Now move forwards into the Collaborate space.

■ What is now possible?

■ How satisfactory might this relationship become? (1 low–10 high)

42 Today to Tomorrow

Technique devised by Fran Burgess

Based on work by Ernest Rossi

You will have come across the use of Rossi's hands approach if you have already visited the techniques in Push and Pull (Recipe 31) and Surviving a Relationship (Recipe 33).

THE INGREDIENTS

The Purpose
Suitable for supporting the process of transition

The Conditions
Time: 10–20 mins
Resources: None
Who: G + E
Skill Level: Easy

The Delivery Method
Kinaesthetic: Hands

The NLP Frames
Neurological: None
Linguistic: None

Here is another application which is very simple and especially effective for a period of transition. Very often we want to move forward. We know what the gains will be. We are ready for the change. Yet there is still a tug that is keeping us back. It doesn't have to be 'All change!' We need to be able to bring into the future some aspects we currently have and value. And we also need to have some sense of how we can finesse the join between the two realities.

This process allows us to form an internal description of the process of change, acknowledge the needs of the present and the future, and accommodate these requirements in a way that rests well with us.

This can be a particularly soothing process, and a great addition to any other preparation work as part of a change journey.

The Technique

1. You are aware that you are on a journey of transition. You may have some sense of what you want to become or where you would like to get to.

   - How confident are you feeling about this transition? (1 low–10 high)

   It is best to show your Explorer in advance what you want them to do, otherwise their eyes will be closed and their actions may not give them the best results.

2. Sitting down comfortably, with your feet on the ground, hold out both of your hands vertically facing each other, about a foot away and about 20–25 cm apart.

   - Allocate the You of Today to your left hand, and the You of Tomorrow to your right hand.

   - Your left hand will pass on to the You of Tomorrow the resources you will need, and hold back those elements which will not prove useful.

   - Your right hand will arrange to receive these.

3. Place your attention on a spot between your hands and wait until you notice both or one hand becoming energised and wanting to move. It may also become warmer, heavier or lighter.

4. Allow this movement to begin naturally, without trying. Be open to any further movement continuing, individually or together, independently or collaboratively, until both hands naturally come to rest in your lap. Make sure that you allow your hands to move spontaneously and freely without exerting any conscious control. You may be surprised at what emerges. Take all the time that you want and need. You may find the movement stops for a while and then gets started again.

5. Become aware of any thoughts that arrive unbidden during the process. You may or may not be aware of what you are specifically bringing to your future – that's OK.

6. When your hands come naturally to rest, check out:

   - How confident are you feeling about this transition? (1 low–10 high)

43 The Song of Change

Technique devised by Fran Burgess

Model devised by James Prochaska

James Prochaska, Professor of Clinical and Health Psychology at the University of Rhode Island, built the Transtheoretical Model of Behaviour Change from over 1,000 interviews with people who were able to give up addictive behaviours independently and unassisted. His research came up with a key finding, namely that taking action was fourth down the line and most interventions didn't take into consideration the first three stages (precontemplation, contemplation and preparation), which accounted for the low success rate of many programmes.

THE INGREDIENTS

The Purpose
Suitable for becoming open to change

The Conditions
Time: 20 mins
Resources: None
Who: E
Skill Level: Easy

The Delivery Method
Kinaesthetic: Spatial anchors
Auditory: Sounds

The NLP Frames
Neurological: None
Linguistic: None

This is such a useful sequential model since it fulfils one of the main requirements of any model – it provides a means of navigation through the problem, both for the Guide and the Explorer. It also requires the successful completion of one stage before moving on to the next.

Your Explorer may be looking at the need to make changes. It may be something physical like over-eating or gambling, or it might be behavioural like constantly finding fault or being self-deprecating. Working from the NLP presupposition that we have all our resources within us, we can use our past experiences of change to direct our efforts now.

For this particular technique I have chosen to go for an auditory approach, which is likely to be less familiar or comfortable for most people, and therefore is useful as a way of introducing something new.

Should your Explorer shy away from this method, you can always revert to expressing the answers in words, gestures or symbols.

20 MIN   E   EASY

The Technique

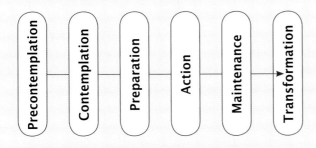

1 Consider something that you have significantly changed in the past, and which is now history. It is likely that the process contained the following stages:

- Precontemplation: When it was someone else's problem and you weren't bothered or you hadn't noticed it.

- Contemplation: When you were prepared to accept you had a problem.

- Preparation: When you began to prepare for what it would be like not to have that problem.

- Action: When you did what you needed to do to overcome that problem.

- Maintenance: When you sustained your activities to make that problem a thing of the past.

- Transformation: When your problem became history.

Make sure you are recording the expression of each stage – literally perhaps – so that if need be you can coach your Explorer to keep his or her discoveries fresh and alive.

2 Identify six places on the floor and step into each space. Take yourself to that point in the journey of change and remember what was happening and what that particular time felt like.

3 Once you have clarity about that time come up with a naturally intuitive sound that somehow speaks for that stage. It could be words (spoken or sung), a rhythm, tune or percussion. It could even be an actual song which sums up the time for you.

4 Once you are satisfied that your sound encapsulates each of the stages, step from stage to stage bringing all the sounds together so that you create a form of joined up music. Prepare yourself for something fascinating!

5 Rehearse your music, adding any extra sounds that come to mind. You might find your body naturally moving to your music – a little dance may emerge!

6 Once you have become familiar with your song, now identify a change that you want to have made. When you have achieved this change:

- What are you feeling and doing?

- What are you thinking and saying?

- What are others seeing and hearing?

7 Place this point at some time in the future. Keeping the Future You very clearly in mind, from the present walk towards the future point, singing your song.

8 Do this five or six times so that the song (and dance) becomes embedded in the process.

44 The Collage of Change

Technique devised by Fran Burgess

Model devised by James Prochaska

This is another way of working with James Prochaska's Transtheoretical Model of Behaviour Change (see Recipe 43) and provides your Explorers with a self-coaching support kit to help them through their journey.

THE INGREDIENTS

The Purpose
Suitable for becoming open to change

The Conditions
Time: 60 mins
Resources: Magazines, pictures, photographs, newspapers, etc.
Who: E
Skill Level: Easy

The Delivery Method
Visual: Collage

The NLP Frames
Neurological: None
Linguistic: None

This time your Explorers are asked to see what each of the six stages (precontemplation, contemplation, preparation, action, maintenance and transformation) means to them, using images, graphics, photos and possible words to illustrate their journey. Invite them to get out their camera or phone and start snapping. Provide or ask them to bring along lots of magazines, pamphlets, internet articles, newspapers and postcards for cutting up.

If they will be working on their own, suggest they put on their favourite music or tune in to their favourite radio station, and to get themselves comfortable where they can spread out and make as much mess as they like. Ask them to write the story of their future in images. As the facilitator, you will have less flexibility if you are doing this as part of a workshop, but you can set up the environment to achieve optimum conditions.

Suggest that they post the resulting collage somewhere it can be seen on a daily basis. This way it will offer its message at an unconscious level. Alternatively, it can become a resource which they can return to time and again, as it continues to talk to them for many different situations.

The Technique

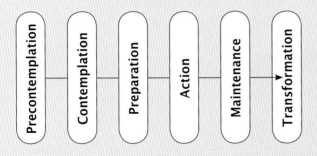

1 Identify a change you want to make or others want you to make.

2 Taking each stage one by one, and with this change in mind, *really* consider what it would be like to be in this stage. Select particular images that for you, connect to this stage.

3 Complete each stage thoroughly before you start making up your collage for the next one, even though you may have lots of images waiting for the other stages.

   Here is an example that a woman exploring her weight might come up with. It is only a suggestion to get your thinking going:

   ■ Precontemplation: Mika – 'Big Girl (You Are Beautiful)', Dawn French, Polynesian women, paintings by Rubens and Renoir, seaside postcards, big women enjoying themselves, lovely rich food, stacked shopping trolleys

   Make sure your Explorers clearly understand that this is just an example and not something to follow.

   ■ Contemplation: obesity graph, furred arteries, heart attack graph, smaller dress sizes, calorie counter of favourite foods, spectators and wall flowers

   ■ Preparation: fashionable shops, beach holidays, food diary, active elderly men and women, pictures of younger thinner you, lots of 'bad' foods and calorie equivalents

   ■ Action: small portions, weighing scales showing reduced weight, cycling holiday, fresh fruit and vegetables, too-big clothes, Oxfam shop for old clothes, shopping basket, slimming club

   ■ Maintenance: piles of lard = weight loss, tape measure marked, restaurant table, size 12 clothes labels, catalogue measurements and order form, passport stamps, awards for swimming, yoga, fencing, dancing school

   ■ Transformation: salsa festival in Brazil, Himalayan trekking, personal health chart

4 Once you have completed your collage for each of the stages to your satisfaction, you may like to scan them into your computer:

   ■ Use them as a screensaver

   ■ Reduce them to credit card size and have them as a reminder in your wallet if you need support

   ■ Have them available on your phone

   ■ Pin them to the fridge

   ■ Stick them onto your calendar either on the wall or on your computer

5 You will begin to notice which phase you have entered into. If you find yourself going back a stage, know that you will go forward again.

45 Breaking Free

Model and technique devised by Fran Burgess

I have had some excellent results using this recipe in my therapeutic practice – when clients come saying they want something in particular and, despite their efforts, it is not happening for them. This suggests there is something holding them back that is outside of their awareness.

THE INGREDIENTS

The Purpose
Suitable for becoming open to change

The Conditions
Time: 20 mins
Resources: None
Who: G + E
Skill Level: Easy

The Delivery Method
Kinaesthetic: Spatial anchors, somatic syntax
Cognitive: Questions

The NLP Frames
Neurological: Submodalities
Linguistic: None

NLP is noted for its action around the concept of ecology, where we test our internal acceptance of a possible decision. How will it affect me, others and the wider world? This is where our 'waters' may say no, but our head so often overrides the signal. This becomes really obvious when we find ourselves repeatedly saying we want to achieve something but never leave first base. Actually, the longer it goes on, the more hopeless and helpless we can feel about it.

There is a simple set of Cartesian coordinates to test this along the lines of: 'If you got this what would you gain? What would you lose? If you didn't get this what will you gain? What will you lose?' I have formalised this effective set of questions into a simple process model.

■ Now: The unsatisfactory current situation where, despite our best efforts, nothing is changing.

■ Goal: This is the desired situation which can have a strong pull to take us towards something better. Sometimes the goal isn't what we really want deep down, which may be the reason holding us back. If this is the case then it needs to be readjusted.

20 MIN

G + E

EASY

■ Limits: This is where we discover the benefits of staying the same, or the elements that we want to make sure we don't lose.

■ Dread: This is what we really don't want and we know if nothing changes this is what we will end up with. The desire to move away from this can be a powerful motivator – as strong as the pull of the goal.

The Technique

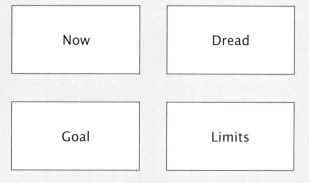

1. Identify a goal that you say you want to achieve but somehow never seem to get there.

2. Set out four spaces:

   ■ Now: your current stuck situation

   ■ Goal: what you say you want

   ■ Limits: what you will lose if you get it

   ■ Dread: what will happen if you don't get your goal

3. Step into each of the squares and become aware of the following. Shake off the state before you move to the next square.

   ■ What are you feeling?

   ■ What body posture or gesture sums up this space?

   ■ What is the shape, size, colour and sound connected with this space?

4. Step into the central point that connects them all.

   ■ Feel the connection between Now and Limits. It often doesn't have much energy attached because of the impasse they create.

   ■ Feel the connection between Goal and Dread. You may find that Dread is stronger than Goal or vice versa.

5. If the pull or push towards the goal is insufficiently strong, then this is an indicator that the goal itself needs to be revisited or dropped.

6. If the push or pull towards the goal is strong, move now to the Limits space.

   ■ What do you have to make sure you bring with you?

   ■ What symbol would represent this? Carry this over into the Goal space and notice what happens.

7. Now stand outside of the whole space and walk around it.

   ■ How do the spaces differ in shape, size, location and colour? How is the Goal space different from the rest?

   ■ What would have to happen to disconnect the Goal space from the others, and allow it to move away from the others?

   ■ Can you do this now?

8. What does the Goal space feel like now?

9. How confident do you feel now about achieving this goal?

46 Box 9

Technique devised by Fran Burgess

Model devised by John McWhirter

John McWhirter takes a different slant on triple description and how to perceive a situation. His focus is on the sender of the message, the receiver and the overall context. He suggests that people place importance on one of these aspects more than the others, and become stressed when desired conditions are not fulfilled.

THE INGREDIENTS

The Purpose
Suitable for discovering which parts of the unknown generates fear

The Conditions
Time: 20 mins
Resources: None
Who: G + E
Skill Level: Medium

The Delivery Method
Kinaesthetic: Spatial anchors, somatic syntax

The NLP Frames
Neurological: Submodalities
Linguistic: None

This is never more true than when we enter into unfamiliar territory, where our confidence will be determined by our response to each aspect. For example:

- **The Knowledge:** Being familiar with what we know and can do, our skills and competence, our effectiveness and useful contribution.

- **The Objects:** Being familiar with the nature of those involved, their culture, needs and responses, our likely reception and the effectiveness of our efforts.

- **The Context:** Being familiar with the context and the conditions of the scenario we are in, the prevailing politics, expectations and desirable solutions, the impact of our actions in the wider scheme of things.

Lack of confidence in any of these areas can create anything from discomfort and stress through to fear and panic.

I have spent many years exploring the relationship between ourselves and not knowing, believing if we could conquer our fear of the unknown, we would become much more confident learners – the ultimate identity to my mind.

John's description suggests that not all the unknown is scary and that different elements will be scarier for different people. So knowing which specific aspects may need additional resourcing would be a godsend. The rest then looks after itself. We may discover that some parts are actually boring and some are positively stimulating!

The Technique

9
Context unfamiliar
Don't have knowledge
Don't know objects

7
Context unfamiliar
Have some knowledge
Don't know objects

8
Context
faintly familiar
Don't have knowledge
Don't know
objects

4
Context
faintly familiar
Have some knowledge
Know some
objects

5
Context familiar
Don't have knowledge
Know some objects

6
Context unfamiliar
Have some knowledge
Know some objects

2
Context
faintly familiar
Have knowledge
Know objects

3
Context familiar
Have some knowledge
Know some objects

1
Context familiar
Have knowledge
Know objects

1   Step into each box.

■ Register your level of wellbeing.

■ Recall a past experience (go as far back as you need to) where this scenario applied, and you survived.

■ What does it feel like? What are you doing? What are you thinking?

■ What does this tell you?

2   Step outside the space and look onto each of the boxes.

■ Which ones seem 'dangerous'? Which ones are 'safe'? Which ones are unimportant?

■ What resources do you need to tackle the 'dangerous' ones?

■ Can you remember a similar situation in the past which you have learnt from?

■ How do the submodalities differ for each box – size, shape, colour? How might you alter these?

3   Gather these resources and step back into the 'dangerous' boxes.

■ What do you now notice?

■ What is now possible?

4   Think of a new situation coming up which would have been scary. Go through each of the boxes and make whatever adjustment you need to make so that you feel equal to whatever this new situation may bring.

47 Letting Go

Technique devised by Fran Burgess

Model devised by Elizabeth Kübler-Ross

The Five Stages of Grief pattern was first introduced by Elisabeth Kübler-Ross in her 1969 book *On Death and Dying*. It is offered as a sequential model; however, in practice it operates more as a process model since not all the stages will be experienced and they will not necessarily follow the order originally offered. Occasionally a so-called 'earlier' stage is revisited more than once. Nevertheless, it is an excellent model to work with, to anticipate loss as well as make sense of the emotions experienced while grieving.

THE INGREDIENTS

The Purpose
Suitable for weathering transitions successfully

The Conditions
Time: 40 mins
Resources: None
Who: E or G + E
Skill Level: Medium

The Delivery Method
Kinaesthetic: Spatial anchors, somatic syntax
Auditory: Sounds

The NLP Frames
Neurological: None
Linguistic: None

We can experience many different types of loss: physical (looks, fertility, limbs, organs, life), mental (job, possessions, career), emotional (independence, relationships, family, aging), spiritual (faith, connection). This loss may be predicted, premature or completely unpremeditated.

This also applies to transitions – first time parenthood, demotion, moving house. It is suggested that the more we can plan for the eventuality of changed circumstances, the more stress-free the transition process can be. Some of us are wired and predisposed to change. Families within the Armed Forces, Consular Services or large multinational organisations develop high thresholds for change and can naturally accommodate high levels of stress due to their habituation to the process. Whilst others have a built-in resistance and reluctance for change, so when it comes it can be particularly traumatic.

In this recipe I have opted to apply the model to a changing identity, since fundamentally I see all loss as an 'attack' on identity. Your Explorers are invited to work with their somatic system. If they can find a secluded space out of earshot, they may like to work with sounds. They will be able to gain an overall sense of their journey through the loss and out the other side to acceptance. Give them as much time as they need to work with this process. You may need to be on hand to offer support.

The Technique

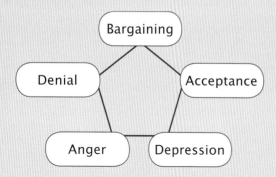

1 Identify a transition you are approaching that you are not sure about. Stand in the middle of the whole space. You may want to set out pieces of paper to mark the five points.

   ■ What is your level of comfort? (1 low–10 high)

2 Face each of the spaces and hear the voices that come from each of them. For example, you might hear:

> These are just some suggestions – make sure Explorers come up with their own.

   ■ Denial: 'I feel fine.' 'This won't be a problem, not to me.'

   ■ Anger: 'Why me? It's not fair!'

   ■ Bargaining: 'Just give me another year. I will accept less money.' 'I won't say anything. Just let me …'

   ■ Depression: 'Why bother?' 'There's no point saying anything.' 'Good guys never get the breaks.'

   ■ Acceptance: 'It's going to be okay.' 'This happens all the time. I'll get through it.' 'Who knows, something good might come out of it.'

3 Selecting your own sequence, move to each space, hear the voices and access a time when you experienced this state.

   ■ Find your body taking up a movement that resonates with this state.

   ■ Let a sound emerge which is in tune with this state and movement.

4 Now allow yourself to move freely within the whole space, incorporating your movements and your sounds in whatever order emerges. Go wherever your feet want to take you.

   ■ Allow your movements to move from big to small and slow to fast, as you wish.

   ■ Allow your sounds to become loud, slow, staccato, high pitched or lyrical, as you wish.

   ■ Allow the space to become wider and bigger, as you wish.

5 Keep on moving until you come to a natural stop. Bring yourself back into the centre of the whole space.

   ■ What is your level of comfort now? (1 low–10 high)

   ■ What is the learning to be taken from here?

   ■ What can you now do with this learning?

48 Game of Life

Technique devised by Fran Burgess

Model devised by Richard Bartle

Richard Bartle developed the Bartle Test of Gamer Psychology in 1996, in which he identified the four main types of players involved in computerised gaming and how they interact. This classification provided significant insight into the design and direction new games could take and has proven to be of enormous use to game producers. After all, it is a huge industry with a lot resting on getting the final product right.

THE INGREDIENTS

The Purpose
Suitable for preparing for a new experience

The Conditions
Time: 30 mins
Resources: None
Who: G + E
Skill Level: Easy

The Delivery Method
Kinaesthetic: Spatial anchors

The NLP Frames
Neurological: Mentors, time, submodalities
Linguistic: Meta Model

The four classes of player are:

- The Achiever (Diamonds): loves targets, high scores, accessing new levels and winning bonuses

- The Explorer (Spades): loves discovering new areas, creating maps and learning about hidden places

- The Socialiser (Hearts): loves creating personalities, interacting with other players or playing a popular game just to talk about it

- The Killer (Clubs): loves destroying things, competing, sizing up strengths and weaknesses and upsetting other players

Now, I've never played a computer game more complex than Spider Solitaire, but I can see how these types could cover the spectrum of activity. It got me to thinking that these archetypes might be a useful gang to have as mentors when setting out in a life game.

Before you get too anxious at the thought of bringing out the killer in you, rest assured that this is the energy that defends and removes toxic or undesirable attacks on your person. As I have worked with clients using this model, it is surprising how frequently this energy is missing or in low supply. It has made a significant difference to them once they have the confidence to up the levels. It is all about taking a stand and asking for self.

I am exceedingly grateful to Professor Bartle for his support and further encouragement. Pacing his continuing developments in this fascinating field of study, I know there are more recipes to come. In the meantime, here's your opportunity to play a virtual game of life, combining the energies of each of the key players, drawing on their wisdom, their focus of attention and their experience.

The Technique

1. Your Spot: Facing Situation, think of a situation that is coming up where you want to have extra resources to support you. Place this situation some distance from you.

   - How confident are you feeling? (1 low–10 high)

   - What does the situation look and sound like from here?

2. Turn around and see the Achiever, the Explorer, the Socialiser and the Killer.

   - What does each of them look like?

   - What is each of them doing?

3. Step into each archetype one by one. Get a sense of what it feels like to take on their energy. Gather up the information each offers you, using this framework of statements:

   - I give you ...

   - I believe ...

   - My symbol for you is ...

   - My fellow archetypes support me by ...

4. Your Spot: Bringing your archetypes with you, step forward into the Situation. Ask each of the archetypes the following questions.

   - What achievements are desirable?

   - What discoveries can be made?

   - What social contacts can be developed?

   - What undesirable elements can be deflected?

5. Now ask yourself:

   - How confident are you feeling? (1 low–10 high)

6. When there is no longer anything further to learn, step even further forward to after this event took place. Looking back:

   - What does the situation look like from here?

   - What do you now know and understand about achieving, exploring, socialising and competing?

49 The Gamer's World

Technique devised by Fran Burgess

Model devised by Richard Bartle

Working more closely with the Bartle Model (see Recipe 48), this technique seeks to clarify what each of the four archetypes (Achiever, Explorer, Socialiser, Killer) mean to us personally and how we choose to deploy them. Many personality profiles suggest that we are naturally predisposed to favour one trait over another and we are stuck with it for the rest of time. To my mind this is a lazy conclusion. I find it more useful to consider developing our flexibility and upping our effectiveness across the board – some which will come easily and others we may need to work at. If we do have a default position, then it is good to know we can come out of it once we've noticed it, should we choose to do so.

THE INGREDIENTS

The Purpose
Suitable for preparing for a new experience

The Conditions
Time: 30 mins
Resources: None
Who: G + E
Skill Level: Easy

The Delivery Method
Kinaesthetic: Spatial anchors
Cognitive: Questions

The NLP Frames
Neurological: Archetypes
Linguistic: None

I have mapped the archetypes against the spectrum of experience – Physical, Emotional, Mental and Spiritual. Some Explorers may underestimate what each archetype could be offering them. They may be using one to the exclusion of the others or they may be limiting their application area for some or all of them.

Here is a chance for your Explorers to expand their world and their impact and influence on it, in a way that feels right, and in line with their values and connects with their sense of purpose. I hope this process awakens excitement and a greater sense of possibility. Who knows what may be brought to life?

This process can be experienced spatially, with the time zones marked out on the floor, or cognitively sitting down. Working in pairs allows the answers to be easily recorded.

The Technique

	Achiever	Explorer	Socialiser	Killer
Physical				
Emotional				
Mental				
Spiritual				

1   Think of an issue or situation coming up which you may have been avoiding but have to deal with.

- What is your level of confidence? (1 low–10 high)

2   You can take each of the archetypes one at a time or you can address all four simultaneously. Either way, answer the following questions:

- Physical: What do you do? What stops you doing more?

- Emotional: What excites you? What do you protect yourself from? What is useful to tell yourself?

- Mental: What do you believe? What is important? What is your highest value here?

- Spiritual: How does this meet your purpose? How are you honouring yourself? What does this bring you?

3   Stand back and view the whole space, mindful of your discoveries.

- What does this information mean to you?

- What is now possible?

- What might you now do differently?

- How might this make a difference?

- Why is this important?

4   Finally, consider the situation that is coming up.

- What is your level of confidence? (1 low–10 high)

50 Building the Team

Technique devised by Fran Burgess

Model devised by Richard Bartle

Following on from Recipes 48 and 49, and taking the Bartle Model even further, this technique looks at how our response to the archetypes of Achiever, Explorer, Socialiser and Killer can change over time, depending on our circumstances and prevailing needs. The levels of some of the traits may be naturally high or low within us, depending on our personality. Some traits may take their default level as a result of decisions and stances we have taken in the past.

THE INGREDIENTS

The Purpose
Suitable for preparing for a new experience

The Conditions
Time: 20–30 mins
Resources: None
Who: E or G + E
Skill Level: Easy

The Delivery Method
Kinaesthetic: Spatial anchors
Cognitive: Questions

The NLP Frames
Neurological: Archetypes, time
Linguistic: None

However, nothing is written in tablets of stone. Nothing is inevitable. When we view a forthcoming event, we don't have to take our current application of that archetype. We have the ability to raise or lower our focus should we choose.

This process allows us to discover that we have an innate flexibility; that we have these resources already within our system; and that we can be at a position of choice regarding how we want to be – even if just in the short term to address a particular situation.

Explorers are asked to investigate their response to these archetypes over four time zones, to discover any changes in response and what may have contributed to this.

They can choose to mark the time zones on the floor or do this technique sitting down. Working with another allows the answers to be easily recorded, but some Explorers report that they appreciate having the time to work on their own. Obviously this will reduce the time allocated to the process.

The Technique

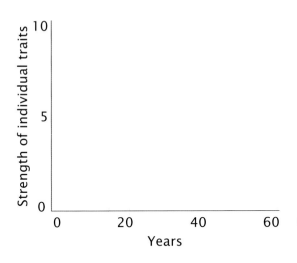

1 Divide your full life into four eras, going back to your childhood and forward into your seventies and beyond. Irrespective of your age, today will fall into one of the first three eras, with an unknown future ahead of you.

2 Now plot a graph for each of the archetypes (Achiever, Explorer, Socialiser and Killer), plot the levels for all four at each stage in your life up to the present time. (1 low–10 high)

3 Looking at the overall picture:

■ What does your graph tell you?

■ Where does each archetype add to, complement or subtract from the others?

■ What have been the downsides and upsides of each?

■ What needs to be strengthened or reduced?

4 With this information, now consider:

■ What have you learnt about your relationship with each of them?

■ How were you controlling, restricting, giving free rein to them?

5 When each of them were at their most effective:

■ What was important to them?

■ How was each of them serving you to the best of their abilities?

■ What influence did you exert to achieve this?

6 Knowing what you now know, continue the graph for each archetype into your future, so that you can predetermine the levels you need in order to deliver your goals and the world you want to give yourself.

■ With this arrangement, what does this make possible?

■ What do you now need to do to ensure that this can happen?

Last Word

I have tested each of these techniques myself. The process took me on an extraordinary personal journey and, when I had completed all of them, I knew I could go through them again as and when a new issue presents itself.

The learning potential within these recipes for you as an individual is tremendous. In the Introduction, you were offered some headings for reviewing. These will help you draw together the themes that are emerging and consolidate the insights you have been gaining.

I have also incorporated many of these techniques into my own training programmes, either because the process provides an outcome which matches the aims of the programme or because the process is an illustration of a particular teaching point – for example, the use of anchors or submodalities or because the process practises a particular skill-set.

In my one-to-one work, having these models at my fingertips gives me choices about how to work with the structure the client is offering. More and more, however, through knowing these models and the possible techniques arising from them, I can customise them to accommodate the client's structure and desired outcomes. I have found them to be equally effective in therapy and in coaching.

Whatever your purpose, I do hope this book has brought NLP thinking and practice alive for you, and you've been able to expand your ideas about what is possible. I hope your experience of these recipes stimulates and whets your appetite for more.

Fran Burgess

Appendix 1:
Modelling Card Sorts

Positive attributes

able	accepting	adaptable
bold	brave	calm
caring	cheerful	clever
complex	confident	dependable
dignified	energetic	extroverted

friendly	giving	happy
helpful	idealistic	independent
ingenious	intelligent	introverted
kind	knowledgeable	logical
loving	mature	modest
nervous	observant	organised
patient	powerful	proud

quiet	reflective	relaxed
religious	responsive	searching
self-assertive	self-conscious	sensible
sentimental	shy	silly
smart	spontaneous	sympathetic
tense	trustworthy	warm
wise	witty	

Negative Attributes

blasé	boastful	brash
callous	chaotic	childish
cold	cowardly	cruel
cynical	distant	dispassionate
dull	embarrassed	foolish
glum	hostile	humourless

ignorant	impatient	imperceptive
inane	inattentive	incompetent
inflexible	insecure	insensitive
intolerant	irrational	irresponsible
lethargic	loud	overdramatic
panicky	passive	predictable
rash	selfish	self-satisfied

simple	smug	stupid
timid	unethical	unhappy
unhelpful	unimaginative	unreliable
vacuous	violent	vulgar
weak	withdrawn	

It Takes Two Card Sort

Sugar and spice	Horse and hounds	Hearts and minds
Horse and cart	Dog and bone	King and country
Ship and sail	Fish and chips	Tom and Jerry
Sea and shore	Tooth and claw	Torvill and Dean
Ducks and drakes	Wood and trees	Bonnie and Clyde
Heads and tails	Fine and dandy	North and south

Gin and tonic	Peaches and cream	Simon and Garfunkel
Top and bottom	Rough and ready	Gamekeeper and poacher

Blanks

Appendix 2:
Quick Reference Table

Delivery Methods

Kinaesthetic: **H** – Hands, **SA** – Spatial Anchors, **SS** – Somatic Syntax, **SSc** – Sliding Scales

Visual: **C** – Collage, **D** – Diagrams, **Dr** – Drawings

Auditory: **GV** – Guided Visualisation, **R** – Reading, **S** – Sounds, **St** – Stories, **W** – Writing

Cognitive: **CS** – Card Sort, **Q** – Questions, **RC** – Relational Constructs

NLP Frames

Linguistic: **CL** – Clean Language, **Me** – Meta Model, **Mi** – Milton Model, **MPr** – Meta Programmes, **NLL** – Neurological Levels, **OF** – Outcome Frame, **SP** – Spatial Predicates, **TP** – Temporal Predicates

Neurological: **An** – Anchoring, **Mn** – Mentors, **MP** – Multiple Perspectives, **NLL** – Neurological Levels, **Mt** – Metaphor, **P/A** – Parts/Archetypes, **S** – Submodalities, **T** – Time

Skill Level

E – Easy, **M** – Medium, **A** – Advanced

Recipe	Delivery method				NLP frames		Skill Level
	Kinaesthetic	Visual	Auditory	Cognitive	Linguistic	Neurological	
State							
1 The State Booster				Q	Me	Mt, Mn	E
2 The State Collage		C			Me	Mt, T	E
3 The Resource Builder	SA					MP, T	M
4 Safety and Vulnerability	SA			RC			M

Recipe	Delivery method				NLP frames		Skill Level
	Kinaesthetic	Visual	Auditory	Cognitive	Linguistic	Neurological	
5 Sad to Glad	SA, SS						E
6 Body Talk			W	Q	Me	MP	E
7 The Accepting Process				Q	Mi		M
8 Total Acceptance	SA					S, MP	M
9 Developing Presence	SA					S	E
10 Building Excellence				RC	MPr, TP	T	E
11 Inspiring a Task	SA				TP		E
12 Modelling Your Anxiety	SA, SSc				TP		A
13 Anxiety Animal Magic	SA					MP, T, Mt	E
14 The A (Anxiety) Team				Q	Me	P/A	M
15 Balance of Power	SA					S	A
16 A Powerful Story			St			MP	E
17 Stuff Happens (Part 1)	SA, SS			RC	Me	S, Mt	M
18 Stuff Happens (Part 2)	SA			Q	Me	S, Mt	A
Behaviours and Skills							
19 It's the Way You See 'Em				Q		S	E
20 Strengthening Performance	SA			Q			E
21 Getting Better	SA			Q	Me, TP	An NLL	E

Recipe	Delivery method				NLP frames		Skill Level
	Kinaesthetic	Visual	Auditory	Cognitive	Linguistic	Neurological	
22 Managing Wellbeing				Q	Me		E
Beliefs							
23 Space Cadet				Q	SP		E
24 Time Traveller				Q	Me, TP	T	E
Identity							
25 Who Am I?				CS			E
26 Role Modelling	SA				NL L	Mn, MP	E
27 Developing a Part		Dr		Q	CL	Mt	M
Goals							
28 Deciding Your Goal				Q	Mi, TP	MP, T	E
29 Finding Purpose			St		Mi		E
30 Aligning Goals				Q	OF	MP	E
31 Push and Pull	H, SS						E
Relationships							
32 Leonardo's Arm			St		Mi	T	E
33 Surviving a Relationship	SS, H				SP, TP	T, MP	A
34 Where Am I Here?			GV		Mi, SP, TP	T, Mt, Space	E
35 It Takes Two				CS		Mt	E
36 Co-aligning Conflict	SA					NL, L, P/A	M

Recipe	Delivery method				NLP frames		Skill Level
	Kinaesthetic	Visual	Auditory	Cognitive	Linguistic	Neurological	
37 Sponsoring Another	SA					An	E
38 Fine Tuning Sponsorship	SSc					S	E
39 Developing Your Inner Coach	SA			RC		P/A	E
40 Conflict Resolution				Q	What, How, Why		E
41 Healthy Compromise	SA			RC			E
Change							
42 Today to Tomorrow	H						E
43 The Song of Change	SA		S				E
44 The Collage of Change		C					E
45 Breaking Free	SA, SS			Q		S	E
46 Box 9	SA, SS					S	M
47 Letting Go	SA, SS		S				M
48 Game of Life	SA				Me	Mn, T, S	E
49 The Gamer's World	SA			Q		P/A	E
50 Building the Team	SA			Q		P/A, T	E

Bibliography

Classic Books

Andreas, Steve and Connirae Andreas (1989). *Heart of the Mind: Engaging Your Inner Power to Change with Neurolinguistic Programming*. Real People Press.

Bandler, Richard (1985). *Using Your Brain: For a Change*. Real People Press.

Bandler, Richard (2008). *Richard Bandler's Guide to Trance-Formation: How to Harness the Power of Hypnosis to Ignite Effortless and Lasting Change*. Health Communications.

Bandler, Richard and John Grinder (1983). *Reframing: Neurolinguistic Programming and the Transformation of Meaning*. Real People Press.

Bandler, Richard and John Grinder (1989). *The Structure of Magic II*. Science and Behavior Books.

Bandler, Richard and John Grinder (1997). *Patterns of Hypnotic Techniques of Milton H. Erickson, MD: Volume 1*. Metamorphous Press.

Bandler, Richard and Will MacDonald (1989). *An Insider's Guide to Sub-Modalities*. Meta Publications.

Charvet, Shelle Rose (1997). *Words That Change Minds: Mastering the Language of Influence* (2nd rev. edn). Kendall/Hunt Publishing Co.

DeLozier, Judith and John Grinder (1995). *Turtles All the Way Down: Prerequisites to Personal Genius*. Metamorphous Press.

Dilts, Robert (1995). *Strategies of Genius: Sigmund Freud, Leonardo da Vinci and Nikola Tesla: Volume 3*. Meta Publications.

Dilts, Robert (2006). *Modeling with NLP*. Meta Publications.

Dilts, Robert, Tim Hallbom and Suzi Smith (1990). *Beliefs: Pathways to Health and Wellbeing*. Metamorphous Press.

Faulkner, Charles, Steve Andreas and the NLP Comprehensive Training Team (1996). *NLP: The New Technology of Achievement*. Nicholas Brealey Publishing.

Gordon, David (1989). *Therapeutic Metaphors: Helping Others through the Looking Glass*. Meta Publications.

Gordon, David and Graham Dawes (2005). *Expanding Your World: Modeling the Structure of Experience* (inc. DVD). David Gordon.

Gordon, David, Michael Lebeau and Leslie Cameron-Bandler (1985). *The Emprint Method: A Guide to Reproducing Competence*. Real People Press.

Grinder, John and Carmen Bostic St Clair (2001). *Whispering in the Wind*. J & C Enterprise.

Lawley, James and Penny Tompkins (2000). *Metaphors in Mind: Transformation through Symbolic Modelling*. Developing Company Press.

O'Hanlon, Bill (2006). *Pathways to Spirituality: Connection, Wholeness, and Possibility for Therapist and Client*. W. W. Norton.

O'Hanlon, Bill (2009). *A Guide to Trance Land: A Practical Handbook of Ericksonian and Solution-Oriented Hypnosis*. W. W. Norton.

Sullivan, Wendy and Judy Rees (2008). *Clean Language: Revealing Metaphors and Opening Minds*. Crown House Publishing.

NLP Introductions

Burton, Kate and Romilla Ready (2010). *Neuro-Linguistic Programming for Dummies* (2nd edn). John Wiley & Sons.

Laborde, Genie Z. (2006). *Influencing with Integrity: Management Skills for Communication and Negotiation*. Crown House Publishing.

Linden, Anné and Kathrin Perutz (2008). *Mindworks: An Introduction to NLP*. Crown House Publishing.

Miller, Philip (2008). *The Really Good Fun Cartoon Book of NLP: A Simple and Graphic(al) Explanation of the Life Toolbox that is NLP*. Crown House Publishing.

O'Connor, Joseph and John Seymour (2003). *Introducing NLP*. Thorsons.

NLP and Applications

Beever, Sue (2009). *Happy Kids Happy You: Using NLP to Bring Out the Best in Ourselves and the Children We Care For*. Crown House Publishing.

Churches, Richard and Roger Terry (2007). *NLP for Teachers: How to be a Highly Effective Teacher*. Crown House Publishing.

Dilts, Robert (1996). *Visionary Leadership Skills: Creating a World to Which People Want to Belong*. Meta Publications.

Garratt, Ted (1999). *Sporting Excellence: Optimising Sports Performance Using NLP*. Crown House Publishing.

Hodgson, David (2009). *The Little Book of Inspirational Teaching Activities: Bringing NLP into the Classroom* (Independent Thinking Series). Crown House Publishing.

Knight, Sue (2009). *NLP at Work: The Essence of Excellence* (3rd edn). Nicholas Brealey Publishing.

O'Connor, Joseph (2001). *NLP and Sports*. Thorsons.

O'Connor, Joseph and Andrea Lages (2004). *Coaching with NLP: How to be a Master Coach*. Element.

Thomson, Garner, Khalid Khan and Richard Bandler (2008*). Magic in Practice: Introducing Medical NLP – The Art and Science of Language in Healing and Health*. Hammersmith Press.

Websites

The following websites are useful sources for NLP and non-NLP articles:

www.anlp.co.uk:
The Association for NLP – a UK membership organisation.

www.nlpu.com:
NLP University, Santa Cruz and the home of Robert Dilts. You will find full listings of his publications and the fabulously comprehensive NLP Encyclopedia.

www.sensorysystems.co.uk/articles.htm:
Articles by John McWhirter.

www.doceo.co.uk:
The fascinating site of educationalist James Atherton.

www.johnbiggs.com.au/solo_taxonomy.html:
Work on the development of the Structure of the Observed Learning Outcome (SOLO) developed by John Biggs and Kevin Collis on classifying learning outcomes.

www.insightkit.com:
To place orders for Insight! cards.

www.professionalguildofnlp.com:
For NLP training providers who you can trust – who value quality, integrity and skills.

Thanks

My thanks go first of all to my major teachers: Judith DeLozier, Robert Dilts, David Gordon, John McWhirter, James Lawley and Penny Tompkins, Bill O'Hanlon and Steve Gilligan.

In particular I am grateful to Judy, Robert, David, Steve and John for their permission to use or modify their work. Also to Professors Richard Bartle, Ken Thomas and Ken Ross from the Elizabeth Kübler Ross Foundation for the rights to refer to their work.

To the members of the Northern School of NLP's Explorer's Club – in particular, Ben Alldred, Chris Ball, Jill Harrison, Lynda Harvey, Jill Leadbetter, Sarah Rhodes and Lynn Sandelance. We spent a year together, tussling with the thinking that finally sorted itself into the simplicity you find here.

To my therapy clients for the opportunity to conceive the new models and methodologies that have emerged out of our explorations.

To everyone who came to the Feeding Frenzy, where each of the techniques were rigorously tested and reviewed.

To David Gordon for his invaluable direction, and for the support and encouragement given by Derek Jackson and Helen Platts.

Index

Image Credits